Motherhood's
Sunshine & Shadows

A Young Mother's Spiritual Quilt

Other books from Ellyn Sanna

All Shall Be Well
A Modern-Language Version of the
Revelation of Julian of Norwich

Following the Mockingjay
30 Days of Devotional Readings
Connecting the Hunger Games Trilogy and Scripture

The Thread
A Novel

Touching God
Experiencing Metaphors for the Divine

Motherhood's
Sunshine & Shadows

A Young Mother's Spiritual Quilt

Ellyn Sanna

ANAMCHARA BOOKS

Anamchara Books
220 Front Street
Vestal, NY 13850
www.anamcharabooks.com

An earlier version was published by Paulist Press as *Motherhood: A Spiritual Journey*.

Printed in the United States of America.
First Printing
9 8 7 6 5 4 3 2 1
Paperback ISBN: 978-1-62524-007-1
ebook ISBN: 978-1-937211-92-9
Library of Congress Control Number: 2013946569

Produced by Vestal Creative Services.
www.vestalcreative.com

*To the three people
who have taught me the most about mothering:
Emily, Gabriel, Micaela,
with love and gratitude forever.*

ACKNOWLEDGMENTS

The Publisher gratefully acknowledges use of the following: Excerpt from "Of Havens," copyright 1966 by May Sarton, from *Collected Poems 1930–1993* by May Sarton. Reprinted by permission of W.W. Norton & Company, Inc. and reprinted from *Recovering: A Journal* by May Sarton, published in Great Britain by The Women's Press Ltd., 1997, 34 Great Sutton Street, London EC1V 0DX UK, used by permission of The Women's Press Ltd. "Christ Came Juggling," copyright 1977 by Eugene Warren (Gene Doty), from Christographia, Cauldron Press, 1977. Reprinted by permission of the author. Excerpt from "Little Gidding" in *Four Quartets*, copyright 1943 by T.S. Eliot and renewed 1971 by Esme Valerie Eliot, reprinted by permission of Harcourt Brace & Company and Faber & Faber Ltd. Excerpt from "To Know the Dark" in *Farming, A Hand Book*, copyright 1978 by Wendell Berry, reprinted by permission of Harcourt Brace & Company. Excerpt from *Circles on the Water* by Marge Piercy, copyright 1982 by Marge Piercy. Reprinted by permission of Alfred A. Knopf, Inc. and the Wallace Literary Agency, Inc. Excerpt from *Mariam: The Little Arab* by Amadee Brunot, copyright 1980 by the Carmel of Maria Regina. Reprinted by permission of the Carmel of Maria Regina. Excerpt from *The Ordinary Way* by Dolores Leckey, copyright 1982 by Dolores Leckey. Reprinted by permission of the author. Excerpt from *The Spiritual Life* by Evelyn Underhill, copyright by Evelyn Underhill. Reprinted by permission of HarperCollins Publishers and Hodder and Stoughton Limited. All scripture quotations, unless otherwise indicated, are taken from the Holy Bible, New International Version®, NIV®. Copyright ©1973, 1978, 1984, 2011 by Biblica, Inc.™ Used by permission of Zondervan. All rights reserved worldwide. www.zondervan. com. The "NIV" and "New International Version" are trademarks registered in the United States Patent and Trademark Office by Biblica, Inc.™ Scripture marked NAS is taken from the NEW AMERICAN STANDARD BIBLE®. Copyright © 1960, 1962,1963,1968,1971,1972,1973,1975,1977,1995 by The Lockman Foundation. Used by permission. Scripture quotations taken from the Amplified® Bible are copyright © 1954, 1958, 1962, 1964, 1965, 1987 by The Lockman Foundation. Used by permission (www.Lockman.org).

Contents

Foreword   9

Introduction
              Sunshine and Shadows:
              A Metaphor for Our Lives   11
Chapter One
              Pregnancy and
              Childbirth: Transformation   21
Chapter Two
              Nourishing an Infant   37
Chapter Three
              Living with Young Children   51
Chapter Four
              Letting Go   69
Chapter Five
              Juggling Act   87
Chapter Six
              Housework   107

Contents

Chapter Seven
Failure   121

Chapter Eight
Discipline   137

Conclusion
Journey's End   151

Notes   164
Select Bibliography   174

FOREWORD

If motherhood is a quilt, then the one I've been stitching has become far wider and longer during the eighteen years since I wrote this book. The toddler whose diaper I changed is now a twenty-year-old. My oldest daughter has just gotten her Master's in Divinity, and my son is a college graduate, out on his own, supporting himself. Being a mother asks far different things of me today from what it did back in the months when I was writing the chapters that follow.

I put off having this book reissued because it seemed to me I should update it: insert all the lessons I've learned since I was a young mother, the lessons taught by parenting adolescents, by sending children off to college, by experiencing an empty nest. I also think and speak of God with a different vocabulary today from the one I used when I was in my thirties. And if I were writing the book today, I'd apply the rich insights from my Jungian studies to the word "shadow." Theologically, I'm not in quite in the same place I was eighteen years ago.

But who's to say where I am is better or "more right" than where I was when I wrote this book? When I spent some time again with these chapters, I realized the book I would write today would be a different one—but what I wrote all those years ago is what is most "true" for the person I was when I wrote it. Ultimately, I decided to leave this book as it was written by the young mother I used to be. The only change I made to this new edition was to remove my gendered language in reference to God.

As an older mother, the quilt metaphor still works for me: motherhood has formed a pattern in my life, a pattern of luminous gold and deep shadow that will be a part of my identity forever. Nothing could really have prepared me for all the things my children's adolescence and young adulthood asked of me—but I had learned the basic patterns a long time ago, during pregnancy and young motherhood. Joy...guilt...the pain of letting go...the struggle to get my own needy ego out of the way...love: the patterns repeat themselves again and again.

This quilt I've stitched will touch the future as well. After all, quilts may fade, their bindings may fray, but their beauty and their functionality endure. They get passed along from generation to generation. Maybe, one day, I'll even use it to make a heavenly bed.

INTRODUCTION

Sunshine and Shadows: A Metaphor for Our Lives

*this quilt might be
the only perfect artifact a woman
would ever see, yet she did not doubt
what we had forgotten, that out of her
potatoes and colic, sawdust and blood
she could create; together, alone.
she seized her time and made new.*

Marge Piercy[1]

If you're familiar with quilting, you'll know that Sunshine and Shadows is the name of an Amish quilt pattern: vivid red, green, and gold squares blazing against jagged black, purple, and navy blue, forming concentric diamonds of light

11

and darkness. The Amish women who first sewed these quilts lived far more simply and austerely than most of us. Like the woman in Marge Piercy's poem, their world was not filled with "perfect artifacts." And yet they understood that the family's worn-out clothes and left-over scraps, the ordinary odds and ends of motherhood, could be sewn together into something both useful and beautiful, both practical for meeting a family's physical needs and symbolic of life's deeper meaning.

Today, we mothers sometimes lose sight of motherhood's creativity and spirituality. We're so busy trying to be everything—both professionals and mothers, good housekeepers and intelligent career women—that our spiritual vision is clouded by exhaustion and frustration. Finding the balance between our roles is hard, perfection is impossible, and the load of guilt we pull onto our shoulders sometimes takes all our energy to carry. But mothering has always been an exhausting life (think about a world without washers, dryers, or permanent press; without vaccines, antibiotics, or Tylenol; without grocery stores, refrigerators, or sliced bread). Despite our exhaustion, we too, like the makers of those quilts, can seize our time and out of the day-to-day ordinary business of living, the "potatoes and colic, sawdust and blood," create something new: something that may even lead us closer to God.

Those Sunshine and Shadow quilts seem to say to us mothers, "Let yourself acknowledge both the light and the dark in your life, the seemingly random bits and pieces of satisfaction and frustration, happiness and guilt, laughter and anger, and you will not only be a better mother in all the physical, practical ways, but you will also gain enough perspective to see the pattern taking shape in your life, repeating cycles of sun and shadow that will lead you into the presence of God."

Sometimes, though, thoughts of God bring us no comfort. Instead, they heap on our heads one more load of guilt. Unlike the saints, who seemed to live uncluttered lives of celibacy and dedication, our lives are filled up with people for whom we are responsible, people who demand constant attention, love, and work. We just don't have time to be holy.

We may not be holy—but we really would like to be perfect. And since perfection is our goal, we have a hard time acknowledging that somber streaks cross our lives as mothers, times of frustration and despair, boredom and rage. After all, our culture paints motherhood in soft, glowing colors. To acknowledge that our own experiences of mothering are not always luminous with tenderness and delight is to acknowledge our own failures, and so we try even harder to be perfect.

But we're swallowing whole the stories our culture tells us, without checking to see if the stories match reality. Like putting on a pair of glasses, the stories have become so much a part of our vision that we forget they're there; we think they're reality itself, instead of the lenses we use to shape our perceptions. One of these stories is that when little girls grow up to become mothers they will be fulfilled and whole and happy. (Wasn't that the happily-ever-after at the end of every fairy tale and paperback romance?) Another story is that of the Good Mother and the Bad Mother.

The Good Mother is always devoted to her children's well-being. Immune to boredom or frustration or loneliness, she constantly centers her attention on her children, instinctively understanding what they need from her. She is the nurturing, ever-loving, ever-patient Madonna, serene and beautiful, shining with God's grace. Her life is lit with sunshine, and she is perfect.

The Bad Mother, on the other hand, hurts her children, whether emotionally or physically. She is selfish and insensitive, and her ego-centered behavior damages her children. She is the witch in our fairy tales, a scary, raging, ugly hag who lives in the shadows.

Well, of course we want to be Good Mothers. After all, we truly love our children, and most of us realize the magnitude of our task. Raising children is likely to be the most important job we'll ever do. Other eras did not put quite the enormous significance on child-rearing we do today, but we are more aware than other generations of how vulnerable a child's emotions are. The sense of responsibility can be daunting, and one more source of guilt.

The guilt comes because none of us are always Good Mothers; sometimes we're a lot more like the Bad Mother. Our love for our children, no matter how deep, is flawed, and those flaws hurt our children and hurt ourselves. When we acknowledge this, our own imperfections loom over us, casting a shadow that's black as night. How can we possibly find our way to God through shadows this deep and dark?

We forget, though, that life comes out of darkness. Look at the seed that lies in the dark ground before it can begin to grow. Look at our own babies who grew in the shadowy interiors of our bodies before they were born into the light. Out of darkness, God creates new life. Even in the shadows, God is with us.

And God does not condemn us for our failures, any more than we scold or punish our toddlers when they totter and stumble. The mother-child relationship is a dyad, and in God's eyes both halves are loved and precious, both equally graced with reflections of the divine. "As a mother comforts her child, so will I comfort you," God says in the book of Isaiah (66:13). In other words, God loves as a mother loves. Our human experience of motherhood reflects the light of God. With all our imperfections, still our mother-love is graced.

But because our natures are only reflections of God's, we will never be perfect mothers; only God can be that. D.W. Winnicott, an expert on child development, talks about the "good enough mother," the mother who, while not perfect, gives her children the basic "stuff" they need to grow and develop.[2] The concept is comforting.

Even good-enough-mothering, however, takes an enormous amount of giving. The level of constant self-sacrifice that motherhood requires is something for which most of us weren't prepared, and to our disappointment we find it doesn't always come easily or naturally. Maybe that's because our world has other stories it tells us, stories that conflict with the Good Mother story, stories about personal independence and our right to do what we want. Having absorbed these stories all our lives, motherhood is supposed to magically transform us into selfless saints when in fact we just weren't trained for being at the demand of our children's relentless needs.

Child-rearing calls for a level of giving that is heroic,

beyond what comes naturally to us, In fact, it's the sort of life the saints knew all about. As much as any religious order, the very essence of mothering is a discipline that can teach us about ourselves and God, a discipline that is as rigorous as any other spiritual path. We do not need to feel guilty because we have no time to take on extra "holy" duties; mothering itself, by its nature, cracks open our selfishness and reveals life's sacred significance.

Our culture's insistence on the Good Mother story denies this fact, nor does it prepare us for our lives' reality. Instead of accepting motherhood's challenge with joy and strength, we cringe with guilt because it is a challenge, because we don't already innately know the wealth of wisdom we can learn in motherhood's sunshine and shadows.

And we do learn in the dark, just as much if not more than we do in the light. When we look at the lives of the saints, we see that God met them in their pain and suffering. If Theresa of Avila had not had her frustrations with the order she founded, if Catherine of Siena had not experienced the failure of her church reforms, if Thérèse of Lisieux had not had to contend with illness and despair, would any of them have experienced God so sharply? If rough clouds of sorrow and loss had not crossed their lives, we would not see as clearly the splendor of God's grace in their lives. Look at Mary. How bright was the sunshine in her life—and how dark the shadow as she watched her son die! Mary, if anyone, understands motherhood's light and darkness.

As mothers, we have three choices; we can try to live only in the sunshine, denying that the shadows in ourselves and in our lives exist (but if we do, we will miss the ways God meets us in the darkness); we can falter in the shadows, overwhelmed with anxieties and our own failures (but then we may miss motherhood's glimmering joy); or we can follow this path through sun and shadow. The challenge is tremendous. Motherhood is no soft, warm place where we can curl up and relax. Instead it is a journey that requires hard work. Like any spiritual path, its discipline is stringent—and its joys are intense.

What This Book Will Not Do

This book will not tell you how to escape the dark side of mothering. Instead, the chapters deal with the spirituality we can find in both the sunshine and the shadows of seven aspects of motherhood: transformation (pregnancy and childbirth), nourishing an infant, living with young children, juggling acts (our many roles as mothers), housework, failure, and discipline. Each section within the chapter opens and closes with a quote, either from the Bible or from a spiritual writing. Quite a few of these quotes come from the writings of the saints. Some of these saints were mothers, some of them not, but whether male or female, celibate or married, they all experienced many of the same trials and joys we as mothers do today.

This book will also not tell you how to deal with motherhood's concrete challenges. In other words, you won't find helpful hints here for toilet training, suggestions on how to organize your house more efficiently, or tips for dealing with sibling rivalry. Many books have been written on all of these subjects, and these how-to books meet a mother's real need for insight and wisdom from outside herself. But that is not the purpose of this book.

What This Book Will Do

I hope this book will help us as mothers gain perspective enough to rise above the seemingly random jumble of our joys and sorrows, high enough so we can catch a glimpse of the pattern being stitched from the everyday pieces of our lives.

Doing that is not only vital for our own growth and development; it also makes our mothering a warmer, more useful thing.

Motherhood is not the happily-ever-after we expected from the fairy tales, a life of safe and cozy comfort. Instead, we as mothers must "seize our time and make new," transforming the sunshine and shadows of our lives into a path that leads us to the only true happily-ever-after: God's presence.

CHAPTER ONE

Pregnancy and Childbirth: Transformation

When our family goes swimming, my husband plunges head-first into the water. My daughter and I, more cautious, creep our way in, first our toes, then our knees, then our hips and stomachs, an inch at a time until at last we are immersed up to our necks, and only then do we duck our heads under the water and begin to swim.

Pregnancy is a little like that. It is a time to inch our way, month by month, into motherhood, a time to acclimate ourselves to this joyful but enormous change in our lives and identities. This is the slow beginning of our motherhood, a time of gradual transformation. Some of us, however, become mothers through different means than pregnancy—with adopted children or stepchildren. This may require my husband's approach to swimming: a sudden dive from one life and identity into another. On the other hand, the long wait for an adopted child may be as full of emotional ups and downs as any pregnancy. The months (and often years) of patience and hope, frustration and despair are as transforming as pregnancy's physical process.

In any case, whether or not we experience pregnancy's inch-by-inch transformation, followed by the climax of childbirth, all of us, by one means or another, eventually make that startling plunge into a new life. We are no longer dabbling our toes, admiring the shining water; we are immersed in it now. We are mothers. Like the early Christians, baptized in a river's cold depth, we too have entered into a brand new identity. We have been transformed.

The word *transformation* means new life, new beginnings, new identities—and all that newness illumines the dullness of our routine existence, helps us see more clearly life's significance, its miraculous joy. But transformation also means the end of what's gone before. For something new to come into being, something else must cease to be. A butterfly can never again be a caterpillar. Its form, its entire identity, has been permanently changed. In other words, transformation not only means new life, it also means death. The butterfly's birth means the end of the caterpillar.

Shadow: The Death of Our Old Identities

Die! Die as the silkworm does...
Teresa of Avila[3]

The death which Saint Teresa was talking about was not physical but spiritual—the death of the self. Four hundred years later, we tend to cringe from words like self-mortification and self-denial. We think instead, in terms of self-awareness and self-actualization. As women, feminism has raised our consciousness, and we are no longer comfortable with the unquestioning self-sacrifice that once characterized femininity. We have a clearer sense of our rights, a firmer belief in our own value. We are unwilling to lose this hard-won self-worth, and Teresa's command to *Die!* is almost repugnant.

But no matter how assertively we have insisted on our independence and strength, pregnancy and childbirth impose vulnerability and weakness on us. Our bodies change, dramatically, drastically, and even when we welcome those changes, pregnancy asserts new limitations on the way we live our lives.

During the first trimester (while our bodies are busy building the placenta, increasing the blood supply, and adjusting to the surges of hormones), we are often exhausted, sick to our stomachs, emotionally fragile. Each woman experiences the traditional "morning sickness" to a greater or lesser degree, but for all of us, this is a time of physical exertion as our bodies begin the enormous task of creating new life. If we have nothing to do except concentrate on this immense and awesome work, then we may see this time as sunlit and joyful, but many of us do not have that luxury. The everyday requirements of our lives—our jobs, our other children's need for care, our many other responsibilities, all the things we once did easily and confidently—may now become nearly too much for our physical strength. These weeks can seem like an endless stretch of gloom.

As we move later into our pregnancies, our bodies may restrict us even more. For the first time we are vulnerable to a host of ailments we never before considered, from high blood pressure to hemorrhoids, varicose veins to heartburn. Even the healthiest of us have to deal with drastic changes in body shape, for in the space of months we increase our weight by twenty to forty percent. We no longer look the same, just as the butterfly no longer looks like a caterpillar. We are not the women we used to be. A part of us has died.

After pregnancy's uneasy twilight, childbirth sometimes seems like a plunge into total night. Birth rips our bodies, breaks us open; its pain and exertion are overwhelming. Lamaze and other natural childbirth techniques may help, as do modern medical options such as spinal blocks and epidurals, but the fact remains: childbirth hurts. Our culture does not prepare us for pain. We do not welcome it. Often, we don't know how to handle it. It frightens us, and under any other circumstances we'd find a way to escape. After nine months of pregnancy, though, we have no choice but to live through this experience, to let it have its way with us, before we can get to the other side where the pain will be gone.

For many of us, childbirth is the first time we become aware of our own mortality. In the midst of labor, we are no longer strong and independent, we no longer even care about our rights. Our professional identities or whatever other self-images have been important to us are gone now, erased by pain. Our only reality is the dark rhythm of our contractions as our bodies struggle to break and burst. Pain penetrates the separation between our minds and our flesh, and in the midst of the experience we are incapable of intellectualizing or sentimentalizing what is happening to us. Instead, we sink deep into the shadows and touch death.

We are not the center of the world as we once supposed. Our needs for comfort and stimulation, for independence and self-determination, have all become secondary. We are forced to set them aside so we can meet the insistent needs of another. Christ's life and crucifixion have been enfleshed in our lives, for we too have accepted the restrictions of vulnerability, just as he did. We have been emptied of ourselves, broken so another might live.

Pregnancy and childbirth impose on our bodies a discipline that is as rigorous as any saint's self-inflicted mortification of the flesh. Teresa of Avila never experienced childbirth, but she, too, had difficulty letting go of her rights, her independence, her sense of herself as an intelligent and attractive woman. She knew she was making no easy request when she told us to die like a silkworm, but she also knew that unless the caterpillar disappears, no butterfly is born. "I am bursting and cannot burst!" Catherine of Siena said of the same spiritual experience.

Catherine never married, never had a child, and yet her words describe the same tension between destruction and creation we mothers experience during pregnancy and birth. Jesus said that a grain of wheat will never grow and produce more seeds unless it first falls to the ground and dies (Jn 12:24). His words remind us that even nature reflects this same principle: new life grows from death. Fertility and fruitfulness have their roots in our brokenness.

"There must be some kind of earthquake within us," says William Law, a spiritual writer of the eighteenth century, "something that must rend and shake us to the bottom,"[4] before the power of the resurrection can be born in our lives. We all have walls we use to protect ourselves, personal boundaries that even our most intimate relationships do not cross, but the growth of a brand new person inside our flesh breaks the very foundations of those walls. The physical demands of this new life send tremors through our being, raze the self-centered structures of our identity, shake our egos at their core.

Without a doubt, sunlight will flood through the broken walls—but that does not erase the earthquake's trauma. Even in Christ's life, though, the crucifixion had to precede the resurrection. Birth and death, growth and loss, are inseparably joined. There is no easy road to transformation.

So should we dismiss today's psychologists with their constant talk of identity and self-actualization? After all, if the saints were right, the greatest growth rises out of death. Maybe we should refuse the new sense of awareness and strength we have today as women and turn back to the old self-sacrificing model of womanhood.

Being selfish, however, is a very different thing from self-actualization (the process of becoming a real self). Remember the children's story, *The Velveteen Rabbit*? In order for the toy rabbit to become a real rabbit, he had to love and be loved—to the point of losing his original, plush identity. Only when he loved enough to be broken and hurt could he become real. And the same is true for mothers. We are not asked to deny our unique personhood, but like the Velveteen Rabbit—and like the saints—we are called to throw away our selfish selves, so that we can become real in ways we have never been before, gaining a whole new identity.

The discipline of pregnancy and childbirth forces upon us the realization that love has more to do with giving than receiving. Our love for this small new life demands that we lay down our very bodies to its service. Our old identities die, unable to withstand love's violence. And out of this darkness, we too are born. We are transformed.

Whoever is bent on saving this temporal life
[comfort and security], shall lose eternal life;
and whoever loses the comfort and security here for My sake,
shall find life everlasting.
Jesus (Mt 16:25, Amplified Bible, alternate version)

Sunshine: The Revelation of New Life

You will see God and be immersed in His Greatness, as the
little silkworm is immersed in its cocoon.

Teresa of Avila[5]

Pregnancy and childbirth may be sunless times of exhaustion and discouragement, or they may be radiant with fulfillment and joy. Either way, they are times of miracle and revelation, times when we mothers experience the concrete meaning of the incarnation revealed within our very bodies. Christ's life united the divine with physical reality—and so can pregnancy.

When a woman is pregnant, her body is the baby's world. The baby has never seen the mother, and yet it is constantly enclosed within her body. So we too are with God. We have never seen him face to face, we may much of the time be totally unaware of him. Yet, like Saint Teresa's silkworm, we are immersed in him. Saint Paul said, "In him we live, and move, and have our being" (Acts 17:28), and the same is true for the baby inside its mother. Paul must have seen the same analogy, for he followed his words with this: "We are his offspring." Only during pregnancy do our offspring experience this total

29

and actual immersion in our physical identity. Mechthild of Magdeburg, the thirteenth-century woman mystic, put it this way: "I am in thee and thou in me, we could not be closer, for we two are fused in one."[6]

Pregnancy helps us understand this fusion, for like the sacraments, it focuses spiritual light so we can see it. One of the definitions of a sacrament is "a physical sign of a spiritual grace." In other words, sacraments bring spiritual reality out from the intangible, intellectual realm into the world of concrete physical experience where we can see and touch and taste. As pregnancy reveals to us the nature of God's love, it too can become sacramental.

Birth mothers, for example, have all felt the fish-like movements within their pregnant bellies as their babies turn and twist, floating in the amniotic fluid. Having had that experience, these words of Catherine of Siena take on a richer and deeper meaning: "Then the soul is in God and God in the soul, just as the fish is in the sea and the sea in the fish."[7] Marie of the Incarnation, a seventeenth-century woman who was both a mystic and a mother, also speaks of this encompassing union. Like the unborn baby who moves and curls serenely within the womb's cushion, we too are always sheltered by God's love. We have no "life or movement except by his life and his movement," says Marie.[8] Mothers who have experienced pregnancy know with their flesh the spiritual reality the saints describe.

And yet our Western culture has tended to separate body and spirit, as though they were two conflicting entities. The intellectual and the spiritual were considered to be loftier, purer, closer to God, while the physical was baser, more sinful, a heavy weight dragging around our spiritual necks. God, however, created physical reality, and when it was made, the Bible says God looked at it and saw that it was good (Gn 1:31). Yes, we live in a fallen and imperfect world, but nevertheless, the physical, tangible world still reflects its Creator. It still is good. Pregnancy reminds us of this fact.

Christ's incarnation also affirmed the goodness of the physical world. The Divine and human flesh became one in Mary's pregnant womb. How could God have done that if our bodies were innately bad and sinful? But still, the thought persists that our bodies are the source of all our sin. As Western women, we often combine this with one more reason for disliking our physical selves: yet another story our culture tells us, this one about slim, Barbie-doll bodies being the only ones that are beautiful. By the time we are adults, many of us have spent a lifetime worrying about whether we are thin enough

31

or pretty enough. With the heavy cultural load we carry, no wonder we often have a cloudy sense of anxiety about our bodies and their worth.

Pregnancy can be like the sunlight bursting through the clouds. Our bodies no longer have to measure up to some artificial set of qualities, for the Barbie-doll standard has become irrelevant now. Pregnancy gives a new meaning to our physical identities, for inside us grows a miracle that exists not in the spiritual realm but firmly in the physical. The artificial split between body and spirit is mended. Within our bodies is the tangible realization of love, a whole new person, an eternal soul fashioned from the fruit of physical union.

What is more, if our ordinary bodies can be transformed and stretched, becoming burgeoning sources of life, then we also catch a glimmer of what may follow death. Speaking of the resurrection of the dead, Saint Paul wrote, "We will all be changed" (1 Cor 15:51). In other words, when we die we shall be transformed. Just as we experience during pregnancy, our old bodies will cease to be so that something new can come into being.

In a book called *Motherhood and God.* Margaret Hebblethwaite compares pregnancy to the resurrection:

Though we cannot imagine it in advance, perhaps when it happens it will have the same feel of rightness and fulfillment, as though the whole development of our earthly bodies has been a sort of puberty preparing us for the moment when in a truly physical way we shall move into a new phase. We shall find our bodies able to do things we never thought they could, a little bit like the way in pregnancy the whole metabolism switches into a new gear, and works bigger and better than ever, nourishing not one but two bodies.... Maybe our risen bodies will have that feel of unexpectedly fulfilled physicality, so that when we materialize and dematerialize (as the risen Christ did) we will feel not less ourselves, but more than ever ourselves.[9]

Martin Luther said something very similar:

At birth a child comes forth amid pain and danger from the narrow dwelling of the mother's womb, into the broad light of day. In a similar way a [person] goes through the narrow gate of death.... And though heaven and earth under which we now live appear so wide, so vast, yet in comparison with the heaven that shall be, it is far narrower and much smaller than is the womb in comparison with the broad expanse of sky.[10]

Childbirth ends our pregnancies, just as death will one day end this life's limitations. When that day comes, when we are born from death's darkness into a brilliance brighter than any we've ever seen, will we experience the same sense of wonder and recognition we feel at our babies' births?

Now we see but a poor reflection;
then we shall see face to face.
Now I know in part, then I shall know fully,
even as I am fully known.
Saint Paul (1 Cor 13:12)

Pregnancy may be a time of joyful, steady radiance, or it may be a time of dark despair, a nine-month night. For most of us, however, the light and shadows are mixed together, both real, like parallel threads in the fabric of our lives. Regardless of whether we are filled with contentment or overwhelmed with depression, the reality is still the same: a new life grows within the hidden darkness of our bodies. Our physical and emotional identities will never again be the same. Like the caterpillar within its dark cocoon, we will emerge from this time changed.

Creation often requires darkness. Think of the natural world, where seeds lie in the dark earth before they grow up into the light. Think of the entire world of darkness that the first chapter of Genesis describes. In that darkness the Spirit of God moved, creating life. Saint John of the Cross speaks of the "dark night of the soul," times of spiritual blindness that are somehow necessary for our growth. Just as birth and death walk hand in hand, so do light and darkness.

Pregnancy and childbirth begin this pattern of sunshine and shadows. Their experience puts us far along our spiritual path, for the disciplines we learn here in motherhood's beginnings are not dispensed with once childbirth is over. Instead, these are lessons we will be asked to remember over and over throughout our lives.

As Christ's followers, we are spiritually pregnant our whole life long, for we are waiting to see God's face, even as we are called to bring forth the Divine into our world. We have opened ourselves to love (just as we did during pregnancy, just as Mary did when she said yes to the angel's message). This opening transforms us and the Promised One is revealed, embodied in our flesh.

CHAPTER TWO

Nourishing an Infant

Once we have our babies, we come home, ecstatic, excited, exhausted, prepared to pick up the threads of our lives. Birth mothers' stretched and torn bodies begin to heal. Adoptive mothers' emotions settle down from the seesaw of hope and fear. We hold in our arms the reality for which we have longed, and we are ready to begin stitching together our new lives as mothers.

As first-time mothers, however, we may be surprised by the reality of post-partum life, for now we are faced with an enormous task: nourishing the baby. Whether we breastfeed or bottlefeed, small babies need to eat often, regardless of day or night, regardless of our own needs. As new mothers we are immersed in this physicality, the constant, relentless demand to provide nourishment.

Given the sheer number of hours involved in this task, it's no wonder this is a time when we mothers can barely manage to shower or run a brush through our hair, let alone attend to our spiritual or intellectual needs. We are sleep-deprived, and if we are birth mothers, our bodies are hormonally out of whack and still far from their pre-pregnancy shapes. So it's also no wonder that during these weeks we are vulnerable to depression and mood swings.

Even so, embedded in our exhaustion and emotional fragility are gleaming moments of joy and tenderness. We are amazed by the perfection of these small new people, and the bonds that form as we feed them fill us with delight.

Still, these are primal bonds, based on hunger, one of the body's simplest requirements. Submerged as we are in our babies' physical neediness, how can we possibly raise our heads high enough above the moment-by-moment corporeal demands of our lives to catch a glimpse of the spiritual world?

Saint Ignatius, the founder of the Jesuits, taught that we can find God in all things. In other words, there is no division between spiritual activities and the rest of life. Instead, as we may have learned during pregnancy, we are constantly immersed in the Divine. God is found in the here and now, whatever that may be.

Whether or not God is visible to us, the Divine is nevertheless an essential part of the piecing of light and dark in these early days of motherhood. And the spiritual disciplines we learn now in this tender, weary time are insights we can carry with us for a lifetime.

Sunshine: Communion

A mother feeds her child with her milk,
but our beloved mother Jesus feeds us with himself.
In tender courtesy he gives us...the most treasured food of life.
Julian of Norwich[11]

Like pregnancy and childbirth, nourishing an infant can be a profoundly sacramental time, a time when the reality of Christ's love is embodied in our own physical lives. As we hold our babies in our arms, feeding them, looking into their eyes as they suck, we experience a communion that is like no other. It is rooted in their neediness and our abundance. The ability to fill our babies' hunger gives us a luminous sense of adequacy and tender competence. The bonds that form now are permanent; they will be threaded through all the long years of mothering that lie ahead.

Psychologists tell us that individuals first learn trust as infants, when their cries of hunger are answered. The boundaries between mother and child are nonexistent from the child's perspective—and sometimes almost equally nonexistent from the mother's viewpoint. Mother and baby are one unit, sewn together with an ever-growing web of dependency and love. No other human relationship is quite the same.

Christ understood that the primal roots of trust are found in the act of nourishment, for he summed up the meaning of his life in the symbolism of his last meal on earth, a meal that the church has formalized into its central sacrament. "Take, eat," Jesus said to his disciples at his last supper, "this is my body which is for you" (Mt 26:26, 1 Cor 11:24). The mother feeding her baby, especially the nursing mother, can uniquely understand the meaning of Christ's words. All of us, like hungry babies, are dependent on God's life for nourishment. Saint Augustine, that most masculine of theologians, made the same analogy: "Even when all is well with me, what am I but a creature suckled on your milk and feeding on yourself, the food that never perishes?"[12] God is the source of all our comfort and delight, and like a mother who smiles at her sucking baby's contented sighs, God delights in our delight. This reciprocal joy is communion's light.

Webster's defines the word *communion* as an act of mutual participation and sharing. This is what the church does during the eucharist. It is also what a mother and child do as the mother nourishes the child. These are acts that knock down our egocentric walls and bind us together. When that happens, not only are we present to each other, but God too is present with us.

Of course, we also associate Christ's crucifixion with the eucharist, for in fact not only his life feeds us, but also his death, his total gift of himself. As mothers, we are not often called to literally die for our babies, but we are asked to lay down our lives. During these early days of motherhood, to a large extent we give up our other occupations, our sleep and recreation, our socialization and careers, and center our activity solely on the needs of these small helpless people. Just as Christ's love required sacrifice, so does ours as mothers.

Sacrifice, however, is another one of those words that are no longer as popular with women as they once were. We tend to connect sacrifice with martyrdom, an unhealthy doormattish sort of attitude. The literal meaning of the word *sacrifice*, though, is *to make holy*. Saint Augustine's definition of sacrifice was "any work done in order to achieve unity with God's holy communion."[13] Saint Thomas Aquinas said that the crucifixion was a sacrifice in that it was an expression of Christ's love for us and for the Creator.

Julian of Norwich, the fourteenth-century mystic, saw how clearly Christ's sacrifice parallels a mother's experience as she nourishes her child. "A mother feeds her child with milk," said Julian, just as "our beloved mother Jesus feeds us with himself."[14] The Bible acknowledges God's mother-love too: "That you may nurse and be satisfied from her consoling breasts," says Isaiah, "that you may drink deeply and be delighted with the abundance and brightness of her glory. For thus says the Lord,...you shall be nursed, you shall be carried on her hip, and be trotted on (God's maternal) knees" (Is 66:11-12, Amplified Bible).

Contrary to what we may have always thought, sacrifice does not mean *to give up or surrender something*. Instead, we must shift our attention in another direction, toward holiness. The root word of *holy* is the same as that of *whole* and *healed*. When we are engaged in the sacrificial nourishing of our babies, we are making them whole and healthy. At the same time we too can be healed, for though the rest of our lives may be on temporary hold during this time, reality becomes one whole piece, the spiritual and the physical. As we see God's love mirrored in our own actions, our tattered faith is mended.

Meanwhile, we may have no time for anything but the most basic personal hygiene. The pile of dirty laundry may rise toward the ceiling, and our interior spirituality may seem non-existent—but our culture's perfect image of the Good Mother is a lie. We do not need a carefully styled body or a neat house or a mind full of complex thoughts and prayers to make ourselves "good." The very nature of our focus on nourishment makes this time holy and significant. We have no need to seek worth in any other activity, for this monumental and sacrificial job is enough. The nourishment we offer our babies nourishes ourselves, illuminating our lives with love. This union, rooted in the reciprocal dependency and adequacy of our physical natures, reflects the radiance of our spiritual communion with a loving God.

> *Our true mother Jesus, who is all love,*
> *bears us into joy and endless living.*
> *Blessed may he be!*
> Julian of Norwich [15]

Shadow: Exhaustion

Lord, my land is dry and parched: send your dew,
My nerves are all on edge.... The hairs of my head are stiff,
all standing straight up and they prick me like needles.
My ears are closed and so dull I cannot hear.
My eyes are on fire, they no longer see the light....
Lord, send Your dew upon this sterile earth.
Mariam Baouardy [16]

I have always been struck by a mother cat's ability to coolly detach herself from her babies. Each time the mother stands up to leave the kittens, they mewl piteously, clinging to her nipples. Their cries pull at my heart, but the mother cat simply leaps from the box, leaving them behind while she goes to eat or prowl or attend to her own grooming. The kittens in their ignorant innocence would rather have a starving, half-dead mother than allow her to go away and feed. The mother cat's hard-hearted indifference to their cries is both necessary and healthy.

Unfortunately, we human mothers have the image of the Good Mother dancing like a sugarplum inside our heads.

Surely, we think, a Good Mother should have a limitless bounty to give to her children. As a result, during these early days of mothering we may spend our store of physical, emotional, and spiritual resources.

Mariam Baouardy was a nineteenth-century Carmelite nun whose experience of spiritual reality was intense and unusual, and yet she was not immune to the effects of physical exhaustion on her spiritual life. No matter how sacramental nourishing an infant may be, the truth is, it's hard to feel spiritual when we are tired. Just as Mariam describes, our nerves are on edge, our hair is dirty and scratchy, our eyes burn. We feel dry, empty, used up.

In a book called *Mother Love, Mother Hate: The Power of Maternal Ambivalence*, Rozsika Parker writes of these feelings of exhaustion and depletion. The intense intimacy between the mother and the baby, she says, the unconscious communication that takes place during the act of nourishment, can bring the mother's own baby-self to the forefront. Union can be blissful and lucent, but when, as mothers, our own personalities are submerged in the needs of the baby, then the natural result is that we, too, will begin to experience a shadowy sense of desperate infantile neediness, for we have depleted our own sense of separateness and strength. "The anguish of a hungry baby's cry becomes your own anguish," says Katherine Gieve in *Balancing Acts: On Being a Mother.* [17]

As a result, these days may be a mother's first experience of guilt, inadequacy, and frustration (but they will surely not be her last). All the stories, all the commercials and greeting cards, lead mothers to expect this to be a shiny, happy time, so when we find ourselves stumbling in the gloom, we assume the fault must be our own. The lovely images of ourselves as perfect mothers, the ones we may have dreamed of all our lives, are wounded. In psychological terms, gaps appear between our egos and our ego ideals.

And into these gaps streams God's grace. The fact is, we are not all-bountiful. We are incapable of being ever-giving, ever-nurturing, for we are only limited human beings with real needs of our own. When our lives become overcast by exhaustion and lack, then we are forced to rely on God, for only God has an endless supply of love and strength.

Yet even now, at the point where we are forced to accept our own limitations, still our babies' need for nourishment is continuous, unrelenting and merciless. We cannot walk away and say, "Sorry, this job is too much to ask of me. I just can't handle it." Somehow, we have to continue to satisfy our babies' hunger.

In the *Spiritual Dialogue* God says to Catherine of Genoa, the married saint of the fifteenth century, "You will love everyone without love."[18] In other words, you will give even when you are empty. Speaking in reference to Catherine, author Carol Lee Flinders says:

> Of our care givers, and ourselves in care-giving roles, I think we expect, ideally at least, something resembling unconditional and unstinting love: the compassion and tenderness, in short, of a mother, a perfect mother. Consciously, we might know this is unrealistic, a child's fantasy of how life ought to be, but the expectation persists and shapes our behavior throughout life. We...feel inadequate when we cannot muster it in ourselves.
>
> The mystic's response—and I think this is Catherine's real point in speaking about love that is "without love"—it is that our dream is not impossible at all. There is nothing infantile or unrealistic about it, for such unconditional love does exist. Our only error is in thinking we can...dish it out *from* ourselves in our present, limited state. The source of such love... is God's love, and once we have tapped into it, it can

pass *through* us to others. To the extent that Catherine has gotten her own feelings and designs entirely out of the way, she is a perfect instrument of a love far more abundant and all-seeing than any she could have mustered on her own. [19]

We should feel no guilt for the days when we nourish our infants automatically, wearily, without tenderness or joy. Even then we are channels for God's grace and love, flowing through us to our children. Our pretty pictures of ourselves have been stripped away, exposing our own primitive and desperate neediness. We are not self-sufficient, as we once supposed; and yet God still uses us. Divine love is abundant and all-sufficient, and God can meet our hunger and quench our thirst.

If you are thirsty, come to me and drink.
Jesus (Jn 7:37, paraphrased)

The blissful radiance of communion and the black anguish of exhaustion seem like they should be contradictory states, as though the one should prevent the other from existing within the same space of time. And yet most of us mothers do experience both during these early months of motherhood, sometimes during the same day, sometimes even the same hour. Both experiences are real and genuine, and both can propel us farther along our spiritual journey.

The reason for the spiritual strength of these experiences, both sunshine and shadow, is that we emerge from them less egotistic than before. We no longer think of ourselves as the glossy center of the world. Communion has broken our egocentric boundaries, and exhaustion has revealed our essential neediness. Less burdened by the selfish weight of our egos, we are freed to travel farther on our spiritual path. We are that much closer to our journeys' end: the God who loves and nourishes us with abundant, tireless love.

✡

CHAPTER THREE

Living with Young Children

We formed tight bonds with our children during the process of nourishing them. When our children are small, these bonds are so snug we have very little space between our own lives and our children's. We are immersed in their being. Their delights fill us with joy; their sadnesses bring tears to our own eyes.

These are days when the morning presence of Big Bird and Mister Rogers are nearly as real to us as to our children. We are as familiar with imaginary friends' idiosyncrasies as we are with our husbands'. Time can be suspended by something as simple as a snowflake, a sparrow, or a garbage truck. And unfortunately, a spilled bowl of Cheerios can upend our own equilibriums as easily as it does our children's.

This intense identification with our children gives us a chance to experience anew childhood's wonder. Our lives are filled with moments of play and spontaneity, simplicity, and confident love. Our dulled vision is washed clean, and we see again life's astounding loveliness, the miracles and beauty that are hidden even in the smallest, most ordinary places. These are glowing experiences, the sort of bright, warm times we always expected when we anticipated motherhood.

We probably didn't expect that we would also identify with our children's selfishness and aggressiveness, their insatiable neediness, their frustration and weakness. Living with children, we are cut off from adult perspectives. Surrounded by demanding little people, we are isolated even from ourselves, from the people we once were. Sometimes we find ourselves screaming with the out-of-control rage of our toddlers' tantrums.

Being childlike is one thing; being childish is something else altogether. We can scarcely recognize the desperate, frustrated, shrieking people we've become. We don't like them. They are certainly not Good Mothers, and yet they are real. Their reality embarrasses us, mortifies us.

The root of *embarrass* is a Latin word meaning *entangle in a noose*, and the root word of *mortify* is the Latin for *dead*. Living with young children can be destructive to our sense of self. It strangles our egos and kills our glib pride in our own abilities. The fact that we can't escape the demands of this life, that we are tied to it by the very threads of our hearts, only adds to our sense of frustration.

However, the saints and mystics all insist that mortification is somehow necessary to our spiritual lives. Just as in the early days of motherhood's transformation, our old selves must be destroyed before new life can grow. "You must be born again," Jesus said (Jn 3:7) and to do that, we first have to learn all over again how to die. Living with children teaches us both how to die and how to be transformed.

Sunshine: Models of Holiness

Beloved [daughter], I will take thee for my pattern
and try to please Him as you please me...
grieve to lose sight of Him for a moment,
fly with joy to meet Him...this is the lesson of love you set me...
give me Grace to copy well this love image.
Elizabeth Seton [20]

Elizabeth Ann Seton was an American woman who founded a community called the Sisters of Charity early in the nineteenth century. She was also the mother of five, and her journal reveals that her spirituality was illumined by living with her children. She understood something most of us mothers know (though we may not verbalize our knowledge): our children are our spiritual directors. Their lives give us a pattern to follow, a "love image" that is uniquely theirs. Immersed in the day-to-day details of their days, we have an opportunity to experience the radiance of their perspective.

When Saint John the Divine wrote his epistles, again and again he called his readers "little children," for he understood that if we are to walk in love as Jesus taught, then we must be childlike. Thérèse of Lisieux, the nineteenth-century Carmelite nun, called her approach to spirituality "the little way"; others have called it "the way of childhood." It is a spirituality that concentrates not on lofty intellectual thoughts, prominent deeds, or elaborate theology, but on living life with a child's moment-by-moment simplicity and love.

As mothers of young children, our lives are filled with tiny twinkling moments: our children's joy at greeting us each morning, the confidence with which they run to us for consolation, their comfort in our presence, and their ability to live in the here and now. All of these give our tired grown-up lives new meaning. Our days brim over with sacramental moments, moments when God's reality is as close and warm as our children's arms around our necks. These moments are un-earned, unscheduled, and free for the taking, as free as grace. By their light, our self-accusations, all the woulds and shoulds and ought-to's, fade away, insignificant and meaningless.

"I should be desolate for having slept during prayertime," writes Saint Thérèse. "Well, I am not desolate.... Little children are just as pleasing to their parents when they are asleep as when they are awake."[21] God's grace is not the stern thing we always thought. Instead, it is as simple and joyful as a child's love for a mother or as a mother's love for a child. We do not have to strive and labor to merit this love: it simply pours down on us, moment by moment, no matter what we are doing. It frees us from the need to achieve, to prove ourselves. Like a child, rocked in a mother's arms, even asleep we are nestled in grace.

"I stinky," my toddler says and holds up her arms to me, smiling confidently. I put off the moment for as long as I can, I must admit, but eventually I scoop her up and lay her on the changing table. As I clean her, she chatters to me about Pooh Bear and Grandma and Daddy-at-work. I shake on powder, then bend and blow on her tummy. She wiggles with delight, beaming up at me; face to face, we smile at each other, ex-change kisses, and I realize that her dirtiness was actually an opportunity for communion between us.

Julian of Norwich says again and again in her writings that we are to have this same attitude of confidence and love toward God—and that we can find the same delight in the Divine presence that our children have in ours. Even our mistakes, our selfishness and failure, can be opportunities for communion with God, she says, if we, like children, "runneth hastily" for help, saying to God, "My kind Mother, my Gracious Mother, my dear worthy Mother, have mercy on me: I have made myself foul."[22] Our recognition of our need for God's cleansing should be as simple, as automatic, as confident as my daughter's "I stinky."

But as adults we don't always even recognize the places where our spirits have been smudged with grime. We take for granted that we think, speak, and act in certain ways. Our children, though, take nothing for granted. The world is shiny new to them, and their vision clear. Their constant questions illumine our lives, glaring on the hidden hypocrisies and prejudices, all our many failures to live as we profess. Motherhood is an all-the-time job. It demands that we look hard at the careless ways we sometimes live, for we can no longer compartmentalize our lives, keeping the doors shut tight on the rooms we'd rather not look at or acknowledge. Instead, our children's scrutiny forces us to wrench open the doors as we struggle to live with an integrity that can withstand their sharp-eyed innocence. Again and again, our arms held up in trust, we must come to God to be cleansed.

Even our vision needs washing, for as adults we have often forgotten how to really see. We are so busy with grown-up responsibilities that we forget to notice the images of grace and mystery imbedded in the ordinary world. Our children remind us.

One day as I stuffed wet laundry into the dryer, preoccupied with the supper I was cooking, the book I was editing, and the phone call I'd just realized I'd forgotten to make, I saw my small son and daughter sitting on the floor beside me, completely still, their faces tilted upward. "Look," my daughter breathed.

They looked as entranced as if they'd caught a glimpse of the Beatific Vision. I looked and I saw nothing, only empty, dusty air. I slammed the dryer door and stepped over them. Then I paused and *really* looked.

The late afternoon light that poured through the window had caught the flying motes of dryer dust, transforming them into a shaft of swirling gold. Each particle glinted with its own fire, a whole universe of tiny, spinning suns. "Is it angel dust?" my son whispered. I sat down on the floor beside my children, and for just a moment I forgot about supper and the book I was editing and the phone call I hadn't made. I forgot everything except the wonder that can turn ordinary laundry lint into a glimpse of heaven.

"The Lord of heaven and earth," says Luke 10:21, chose to reveal the mysteries of himself to children. As William Blake says in *Songs of Innocence*, children are able

> To see a world in a grain of sand
> And heaven in a wild flower,
> To hold infinity in the palm of your hand
> And eternity in an hour.[23]

When we live so closely with them, our lives bound tight together, sometimes we get to see with our children's eyes.

And more than anything, children see with the eyes of love. As Saint John tells us, perfect love casts out fear (1 Jn 4:18), and as we learn from our children's trusting love, we see even our grown-up anxieties with new eyes. Elizabeth Seton writes of getting up in the night to wake her child from a nightmare. Her child opened her eyes to find herself in her mother's arms, and "so it will be with me when I die, I will awake from all my fears and be with God."[24]

Truly I say to you,
whoever does not receive the kingdom if God like a little child
shall not enter it at all.
Jesus (Mk 10:15 NAS)

Shadow: Mortification

I no longer belong to myself.
Some evenings, after being worn out by others,
I do not know who I am. I am someone else.
Mother Teresa of Calcutta [25]

As mothers living with young children, we experience many moments of delight and wonder—but we often stagger through our days without even the faintest glimmer of self-knowledge. Like Mother Teresa, who gave her life to work with India's poor, we are inundated with the needs of others and we have no time for reflection or awareness. We simply do what has to be done. And when the last diaper has been changed, the last load of laundry washed, the last lullaby sung, we fall into our own beds, exhausted. We have no time for ourselves.

The neglected parts of who we are begin to shrivel and droop, like leaves on a plant in a dark room. Something inside us is dying. When we have a moment to think about this death, we resent it. Some days this fading, frustrated self screams for attention as loudly and childishly as do our children. If we could meet our children's needs with sweet, self-sacrificing patience, then maybe we could use our new halos to light our lives. Instead, our helpless rage is just one more noxious germ attacking our weak self-confidence, for a Good Mother would surely be more patient, less resentful, more consistent in her enjoyment of her children's presence. Our failure to be Good Mothers strikes a wound at our drooping egos, a wound we try to hide while it oozes with infection.

One of Webster's definitions for mortification is "putrification, necrosis, gangrene." If we must die to ourselves, why can't the death be swift and sharp—a clean, dramatic end to our selfishness—instead of this slow, exhausting rot that eats away at our old identities? Of all the spiritual disciplines, mortification is probably the least attractive, for how can putrification produce health?

But according to Evelyn Underhill, an English spiritual author, mortification is necessary to our spiritual lives because dealing with ourselves is a slow but necessary process. It means, she says, "killing the very roots of self-love, pride and possessiveness, anger and violence, ambition and greed in all their disguises, however respectable."[26]

Nothing digs at our selfish roots like living with young children. When the saints practiced mortification they abstained from earthly pleasures and human satisfactions; they denied themselves comfort. In our modern world, few people follow this peculiar spiritual path, and yet motherhood requires that we, like the saints, mortify our senses by exposing our eyes, ears, and noses to constant disorder and confusion. We abstain from intellectual pursuits and often postpone our professional goals. We deny ourselves the comfort of other adults' companionship. Our lives are cloistered within the four walls of our houses, buried in the depths of our children's needs.

Recently, I complained to a group of women that Christ failed to give me a spiritual model I could relate to as a mother, since he was, after all, a man. Since then, however, as I read the Gospels I am struck by the similarities between Christ's life and mine. Like us mothers, he was a nurturer, a healer, a teacher. He, too, struggled to balance the demands of his active life while being responsible for the spiritual needs of his "family" of twelve. And like us, no matter how hard he tried to

61

find some time to be alone, people were always following him, wanting something from him.

As mothers, we can seldom even go to the bathroom by ourselves without finding we have an audience of little people, waiting for us to be done so we can do something for them. There is no escaping their demands. They are always pulling at us, hanging on us, wanting something. Our old names are gone now and we all have the same new name: Mommy—and when we hear it, we often think, "What do they want from me now?"

Elizabeth of the Trinity, a nineteenth-century nun, knew how this feels, for she wrote, "I am isolated from, separated from, stripped of myself."[27] This loss of our own identities is a frightening feeling. Surrounded constantly by our children, we are lonely, yearning for our old lives, our adult friends, our lost selves. We are accustomed to thinking of solitude as a time for self-reflection and growth, but the loneliness we experience now does not feel constructive in any way.

"Settle yourself in solitude," advises Teresa of Avila, "and you will come upon Him in yourself." [28] We picture her sitting quietly in some empty, silent cathedral, her hands peacefully folded. It's a comfortable image, an image that's in stark contrast to a mother's hectic life. As mothers, how can we come upon God in ourselves when we're so busy meeting our children's demands? How can we possibly "settle" ourselves when our days are filled with hectic noise and frantic busyness, especially when our own voices are sometimes the loudest and most frantic? Oh, we can find God in our Good Mother moments, those times when living with our children fills us with sacramental joy, but not here in the darkness of our own decaying egos. And yet the psalmist assures us that we *can* find him even here. Even in death's shadow he is with us (Ps 23:4).

What's more, according to the mystics this uneasy loneliness is the very thing our spiritual lives require if they're to grow. "Solitude," writes Thomas Merton, "means being lonely not in a way that pleases you but in a way that frightens and empties you to the extent that it means being exiled even from yourself." [29] Not a pleasant condition by any means, but this state of exile is necessary. Otherwise, we will stroke our own egos till they form a hard shiny shell that's impervious to God's grace. Solitude is not meant to be comfortable.

And Teresa of Avila did not find it a comfortable thing either. She spent very little of her life alone in serene silence. Instead, like Mother Teresa of Calcutta, she learned to recognize God "even in the guise of the fretful, the demanding, the unreasonable." [30] Sometimes we, too, manage to catch glimpses of God's face in our children's fretful demands. The challenge is greater to see him in our own irrational anger. And yet he is there with us.

Thomas Merton assures us that

> Solitude is not found so much by looking outside the boundaries of your dwelling, as by staying within. Solitude is not something you must hope for in the future. Rather, it is a deepening of the present, and unless you look for it in the present you will never find it. [31]

In other words, we can't put off our spiritual growth for another day—a day when we have more time, a day when we can finally have some peace and quiet all to ourselves. Instead, we must somehow recognize God's face in the midst of dirty diapers and peanut butter sandwiches and quarreling children.

Sometimes, however, we need to exercise our imaginations if we're to see Jesus sitting with us among the chaos. Our powers of make-believe may have nearly atrophied from lack of use (after all, it's a talent we discarded when we entered the grown-up "real" world), but exercise will make them stronger.

In the sunlit moments of living with our children, we learn how to play again, how to pretend. Now, among the shadows, we can use our imagination's strength to lift us above ourselves, high enough that we can again peek into the spiritual world.

Catherine of Siena realized the imagination's creative power. As a young woman living in the fourteenth century, her one longing was to become a nun, to enter a cell where she could be alone with God. Instead, she lived with her parents and her nine brothers and sisters, at their constant beck and call, without even the privacy of her own room. Inside her heart and mind, writes her friend and biographer, Raymond of Capua, she constructed for herself "a secret cell...an inner cell which no one could take away from her."[32] Occupied with the noisy external demands of her large family, she still continued to grow more and more intent on her inner vision of God's love—her well-exercised, mature imagination helped her do it.

"As I could not make reflection with my understanding, I contrived to picture Christ within me," said Saint Teresa.[33] Sometimes we have to let our intellect drop and make believe we see Jesus even when we don't. Pretending is okay. As any child knows, make-believe helps us reach higher, run faster, even see more clearly that which our physical and intellectual vision can't comprehend. "A day filled with noise and voices can be a day of silence, if the noises become for us the echo of the presence of God, if the voices are, for us, the messages and solicitation of God," Catherine de Hueck Doherty writes in her book *Poustinia: Christian Spirituality of the East for Western Man*.[34]

Doherty writes of our culture's need for "desert times," when we withdraw from the rest of the world, from the rest of our lives. These times may occur in silence and solitude, as they did for Christ when he withdrew into the desert before he began his official ministry, or they may be like Catherine of Siena's "desert," a time when she secluded herself within her father's noisy, crowded house. Either way, these lonely times strengthen us.

We need to remember, though, that the desert times do not last forever. Christ fasted in the wilderness for forty days, not his whole lifetime. Catherine of Siena did not live in the hectic obscurity of her father's house forever, but went on to become an ambassador for peace who persuaded the Pope to return from Avignon to Rome. Our days of living with young children will also be over all too soon. Buried in mortification's gloom, we lose our sense of time. The days seem never-ending, with no relief in sight. We too, however, will one day go on to do something else.

But without his time of testing and withdrawal, Christ's ministry would not have been the same, just as Catherine of Siena would not have become a great woman of action without the strength she built in her years of secluded mortification. "For a soul who is not thus destroyed and freed from itself," writes Elizabeth of the Trinity, "will of necessity be trivial and natural at certain times.... [But] then she will live in the eternal present where [God] lives."[35]

Though we cannot see it now (for grace is invisible), we will emerge from this time stronger, more able to live in God's eternal present. Life shoots greenest from the mulch of last year's rotten leaves, and we too will one day spring forth from our mortification, alive and new.

The heavenly Bread which [the saints] were given was given to make them strong..., not because it tasted nice. Great courage and initiative, the hardy endurance of privation and fatigue...are

at least as characteristic of them as any of the outward marks of piety. So too their inner life, which we are inclined to think of as a constant succession of spiritual delights, was often hard and painful. Willingly and perpetually, they prayed from within the Cross, shared the agony, darkness, loneliness of the Cross; and... shared in its saving power.

Evelyn Underhill [36]

During this stage of motherhood's spiritual path we swing from delight to frustration, creativity to exhaustion. We want so much to walk only in the light of these days, but sunbeams cannot be caught. They slip through our fingers, leaving our hands empty in the dark. And yet one way or another, living with children opens wide the doors inside our hearts. Some of these doors reveal glimpses of heaven's hope and light; some show us only our own dim loneliness. Some open into the bright mystery of the world around us, while others open into our murky interior selves. But wherever the doors lead, as long as they are open, we are free to move forward on our spiritual path, free to explore and grow and learn. And God, the only Perfect Mother, is free to come in.

CHAPTER FOUR

Letting Go

This chapter would seem to belong at the end of the book. After all, during the early stages of mothering, our lives are all about closeness and connection, about bonds of love so tight they nearly strangle. In one sense that's true, but in another sense motherhood's reality is about letting go and separation.

From birth on, motherhood is a sequence of letting go. In fact, birth is the most dramatic of all separations, for we go from being truly one flesh with our children, to being two separate physical entities. The umbilical cord is cut, and we are no longer one. The intensity of nourishing a baby, however, often hides from us the truth of birth's drastic separation, and sometimes weaning is the first time we realize we are not one with our children after all. Especially if we breastfeed our babies, weaning lets us experience again our own sense of separateness and aloneness. We may find ourselves taking a deep breath of relief—followed by an equally deep breath of sadness and loss. But living with young children demands so much of our attention that we often quickly forget that sense of release and loneliness. The first time we leave our children at day care, however, or the first time we take them to nursery school or kindergarten, we will find ourselves once again heaving sighs full of ambivalence. We desperately need some time to ourselves, and yet we hate to see our children leave us.

As our children enter grade school, they separate still further, further still during adolescence. They no longer hold our hands while they cross the street. They no longer run to us for comfort. Eventually they will no longer even live in the same house with us. The process of separation is long and slow, more gradual even than pregnancy, and its achievement is more difficult and complicated than birth—and often just as painful.

We can refuse to let go, refuse to let the pain have its way with us. We can make our children our possessions, living our lives through them, sinking into martyrdom and resentment— or we can accept the gifts of relief and release that separation gives us. As mothers, we have the same chance as our children to become more individuated now, more uniquely our own people.

This is one section of motherhood's path, however, when we often choose to walk in the shadows rather than step out into the light.

Sunshine: Rest and Relief

O that I had wings like a dove! I would fly away and be at rest.
Psalm 55:6

Traveling in the car with my family, all of us packed in together (my daughter complaining because her brother's elbow is touching her, my son whining that his sister is pushing him, the baby whimpering because she dropped her bunny, and me singing songs and telling stories to keep everybody happy, while my husband drives), sometimes I have a totally irrational fantasy: the car door is suddenly sucked open and I'm whooshed out into the air. The wind carries me higher and higher, my children's clamoring voices grow fainter and fainter below me, and at last I'm far above the earth. Floating in the silent sunshine, I relax, freed from all my responsibilities.

The intensity of motherhood's demands inspires fantasies like this. We love our children, but oh, if we could only have a few minutes to ourselves, to rest, to think, to do something else for just a little while.

Fortunately, motherhood's responsibilities are not as constant and never ending as they sometimes seem. Gradually, our children separate from us, become more independent. Day by day, they need us less intensely. Just when we think we can't possibly stagger out of bed one more night to feed them, we wake up one morning to find they've slept eight hours without eating (and we run into their rooms to make sure they're still alive). When our arms and backs are aching from carrying babies, then all at once they learn to walk for themselves. And when we think we'll never have another moment that's all our own, we discover from one day to the next our children have gone off to school, to their friends' houses, and then eventually to college. Our eyes have grown so used to shadows that the sudden light makes us blink, and then we realize: we can read books, go shopping, spend time with our husbands, talk to friends, pursue our careers—without being interrupted. Our lives have been given back to us.

It seems too good to be true, when we've become so accustomed to the dark discipline of work and responsibility. But over and over again in the Bible, God speaks of the necessity for times of rest. Just as all good parents model the behavior they want from their children, so in the book of Genesis, God models a healthy pattern for us by resting on the seventh day after creation. Hebrews 4:9 says, "There remains, then, a Sabbath rest for the people of God." Jesus promises, "Come to me all who are weary and burdened, and I will give you rest" (Mt 11:28). God knows how much we need these times of relaxation and restoration, for just as a mother understands her children's limitations, so does Divine compassion encompass us. God knows how we're made and what we need; God "knows our frame" (Ps 103:14).

And our physical frame needs these times of relief as much as our emotions do. Sometimes, though, the days don't seem to have enough hours in them, and we're tempted to carve out time from our sleep, that small Sabbath space we're granted every night. But Teresa of Avila reminds us, "For the love of God, look at the thing from another point of view, and stop devoting the hours you ought to be asleep to either making plans—or even to prayer." Later, she adds, "We need to treat our bodies well so as not to wreck the spirit.... God prefers your health and obedience to your penances."[37] These Sabbath times are not to be refused out of a false sense of either competence or self-sacrifice. Instead, if we are obedient, we will "make every effort to enter that rest" (Heb 4:11).

Piece by piece, our lives are given back to us, but they can never be the same as they were before. The sunshine and shadow of motherhood's disciplines are transforming us. We no longer belong only to ourselves, and what we do with our moments of rest and respite will be shaped by who we have become. Historically, God's people have always connected Sabbath times with worship. When we have time to rest, we also have time to think consciously about God and offer up our love.

In his book *The Celebration of Discipline*, Richard Foster defines worship as "breaking into the Shekinah of God."[38] *Shekinah* is a Hebrew word, feminine in form, for God's immediate presence in the world. I like to think that these Sabbath times are the "quality time" that God, our Good Mother, gives to us, times to relax and delight with the Divine presence, just as our children do with us. "The Lord thy God," says the prophet Zephaniah, "will rejoice over thee with joy; he will rest in his love, he will joy over thee with singing" (Zeph 3:17 KJV).

On the other hand, we can choose to use our moments of rest and relief to retreat back into our comfortable and familiar selfishness. But that would mean wasting the hard discipline we've passed through already. It would mean turning our backs on the unlimited space and light of Shekinah, and choosing instead the tight dark walls of our own egos.

Margery Kempe, a fifteenth-century mother of fourteen children, heard Jesus say to her. "If you allow me to rest in your heart on earth, then believe me when I tell you that you will rest with me in heaven."[39] Just as Christ was present in transformation and mortification, in communion and frustration, so too, the Divine can be present in something as simple as resting—and when we find God there, these small spaces of relief are illumined by eternity.

The eighteenth-century theologian John Wesley said that even during our leisure times, even when we are lying down, we can still walk with God continually, seeing the One who "is invisible" with the "loving eye" of our minds.[40]

He makes me lie down in green pastures;
He leads me beside quiet waters.
He restores my soul.
Psalm 23:2,3

Shadow: Separation Anxiety

It often happens
that the devil urges a soul to excessive penances to tire her
and render her unfit for the service of God
and the fulfillment of her duties.
Anna Maria Taigi[41]

The ancient Greeks told a story about a mother who was forced to let go of her daughter. Persephone, like many children, wandered away from her mother and from her mother's sphere of power. The girl was picking flowers, an innocent-seeming pastime, but the myth says that one of the flowers she picked was the narcissus. Often our narcissism, our ego-love, makes us susceptible to danger. Sure enough, as Persephone reached for yet another narcissus, the earth opened up, and Hades, the Lord of the Underworld, grabbed hold of her.

When Demeter, Persephone's mother, heard that her daughter was gone, she went into mourning. She stopped eating, she stopped grooming herself, she abandoned all her normal affairs, and became obsessed with Persephone's predicament. She was immersed in Persephone's life, with no life of her own. She certainly did not welcome her new freedom from responsibility, nor did she take advantage of her aloneness as a time of holy rest. Instead, as Blessed Anna Maria Taigi says, she took on "excessive penances" that both tired her out and made her unable to fulfill her other responsibilities.

At last, however, Demeter did manage to take up an occupation of sorts, though it lacked the strength and creativity of her old work. She became a caretaker for a human child. In this role, she had enough distance from the child to know what he truly needed. Her own emotions were not tied to him the way they were to Persephone, and so each night she put the little boy into a magic fire to make him immortal. When the boy's mother saw what Demeter was doing, she was understandably upset, but Demeter said. "You don't know what is really good for your child."

Eventually, Demeter worked out a compromise that allowed her to have Persephone half the year, but she never resigned herself to her daughter's loss during the remainder of the year. Each time she was separated from Persephone, she again went into mourning and abandoned her creative work. She was never able to achieve enough sense of separateness and individuality to allow her own child to be thrust into the fire; just like the human mother she rebuked, she too was convinced she knew best what was good for her child.

As mothers, we are often, like Demeter, asked to let go of our children and accept that what looks dangerous from our point of view may, from God's perspective, be what our children need. Sometimes this means allowing them to stay overnight for the first time at Grandma's house. Sometimes it means letting them get their driver's license. Sometimes it may even mean standing back while they face hurt and failure. Motherhood is about nurturing our children not only in human ways but also in divine ways. Sooner or later God requires that our children pass through the fire, that they may become the whole selves they were created to be. Complete mothering, mothering that has died to selfishness, demands that we allow our children to be separate from ourselves.

This separation doesn't come automatically, though. Our culture expects the impossible of mothers: we are supposed to be one with our children and we are supposed to "cut the apron strings." To accomplish this paradox, we sometimes take on the role of self-sacrificing martyr: we will let our children go free, while we continue to be one with someone who is leaving us. Our own lives as mothers are shrinking, and so we devote ourselves to reflecting our children's lives. No wonder, then, that we find ourselves resenting our children's freedom, trying to limit it in covert ways so we can still maintain control. Our children's growing independence offers us chances to rest, to regain our own sense of who we are, to pursue other occupations—but we shake our heads and turn away.

Anna Maria Taigi, a nineteenth-century mother of seven children, understood the difficulty we mothers have accepting these gifts of rest, relief, and release. After all, release means to let go—and we don't want to. Letting go is scary, and we feel guilty even thinking about it. That guilt is one of our soul's "excessive penances" that tire us out. But after all, we're *supposed* to be one with our children. We learned that primary lesson with blood and pain, milk and exhaustion. So how can God (or our children) expect us to unlearn it now?

Psychologists tell us that each stage of children's development involves them in a conflict between self and other. The same is true for mothers, for motherhood and childhood do not exist independently. They are reciprocal, mirror images of each other. As mothers, separation fills us with guilt—and our children reinforce that guilt, for part of them experiences separation from us as rejection. Yet we too feel rejected when our children no longer need us. Children (especially two-year-olds and adolescents) rage against their powerlessness, their lack of autonomy. We mothers also rage as we see our control of their lives slipping between our fingers. They betray us by wanting to be free. As mothers, we betray *them* no matter what we do, whether we hold them back or let them go.

Part of us wants them gone, wants to be free. We have not totally died to our egocentric, ambitious selves, and like starved tigers prowling restlessly inside our hearts, those old identities prick up their ears when the cage creaks open. At the same time, though, we realize that the world outside motherhood's safe confines is a dangerous one, especially for our children. If we let them go, then we risk losing our children to forces and influences beyond our control. And anyway, our wild, selfish selves were meant to die, so surely we'd be wrong to listen to their muttering growls. Motherhood is about dying to self, that's the lesson we've all learned, and so if freedom is thrust upon us, we'll accept it only as another blow to our identities, with a sense of martyrdom and carefully preserved hurt.

What a tangled welter of emotions! To hide our guilty ambivalence, children and mothers both sometimes cling even harder to each other, cloaking their confusion with anxiety whenever separation is necessary. And yet, says author Rozsika Parker, even our cloudy ambivalence and anxiety can be creative and fruitful. Without them, we would certainly be more comfortable; we might even curl up and bask in motherhood's sunshine like contented cats. But we would not become conscious of our separateness, we would not examine our own hearts, and we would not grow.

In other words, we don't have to listen to our guilty feelings. Proverbs 16:25 says, "There is a way that seems right, but in the end it leads to death." Tying ourselves to our children is such a way. If children are to develop their own sense of autonomy and self, then right from the beginning, we as mothers must give them the experience of relating with a complete and separate person. Jessica Benjamin, author of *The Bonds of Love*, says "only a mother who feels entitled to be a person in her own right can ever be seen as such by her child," and only such a mother will be able to "set limits to the inevitable aggression and anxiety that accompany a child's growing independence."[42] When we bind ourselves to our children's lives, we may hinder them on their path to holiness and wholeness—and we will definitely hinder ourselves.

Loosing these bonds does not mean that our love is diminished. We do better, though, when we *feel for* our children than when we *feel one* with them. Our love helps us empathize with our children, to imagine their feelings, but those feelings are nevertheless separate from our own. When we are blind to the boundary line between ourselves and our children, then we are more likely to trespass on their God-given individuality and we are less able to reach out to them, with our own selves intact, and be of help.

In her book *The Ordinary Way*, Dolores Leckey quotes a poem written by a mother whose son is dying:

Dying takes a lifetime—and this dying will take two lifetimes—

Yours and the child's. But his dying, like all men's, will be his alone and uniquely. You are the watcher, the occasional comforter (...never knowing if your words help);

The lived reality so much more powerful than imagined ones. Powerful in the sense that all suffering enlarges one's heart. [43]

Most of us, thankfully, are not called to watch our children's physical deaths (though some of us will), but we all have to accept the riskiness of their mortality. When we let go of our children, this is part of the package. Our anxieties are not all imaginary. The truth is, our world is a dangerous and uncertain place. When the time comes, however, for our children to confront their limitations, to take risks, to experience loss, we will be able to offer comfort and help only if we are separate from them, not immersed over our heads in their experiences.

In the Old Testament, Abraham was another parent who was asked to put his child in the fire. God eventually made clear that Abraham was not meant to literally sacrifice Isaac, but nevertheless Abraham demonstrated his total, unflinching confidence in God.

Like Abraham, we too are called to let go of our children, releasing them into God's hands. God's demand for Abraham to sacrifice his son seems heartless to us, and when God asks us to allow our own children to suffer, the request feels just as harsh. Our hearts may be enlarged—but who wants to grow at the cost of our children's pain?

Mary, the mother of Jesus, is sometimes called the *mater dolorosa*, the sorrowing mother who allowed her child to suffer. And Christ had another Parent who watched from heaven as a beloved child died in agony. In other words, we are not alone in our pain as we let go of our children, allowing them to be sacrificed, allowing them to be made holy. God has experienced this same pain; the Divine presence is here with us in it.

Sometimes, though, we find we can trust God for our own lives more easily than we can for our children's. To watch our children's gradual separation from our protection and care radically tests our faith in God's reality, but if we truly believe that God's grace is real and active, then we must believe it is equally real and equally active in our children's lives.

Julian of Norwich said, "God...wills that we should...give up our senseless worrying and faithless fear...He wills that we should quickly turn to him."[44] Worrying comes easily to mothers, though. It's hard to let go, but the most often repeated commandment in the Bible is "Fear not!" Fear makes us cling. It weighs us down and it slows our progress on motherhood's spiritual path.

Faith lets go.

Wherever a mother...turns, unless she turns to you, she clasps sorrow to her heart.... Children do not last.... Indeed, we cannot lay firm hold on them even when they are with us.... Let me praise you for my children, my God who made them all, but do not let the love of them be like glue to fix them to my heart.

(Adapted from a prayer of Saint Augustine. [45])

Letting go is hard. As mothers, we too must be weaned, from the gratification of being needed and important and in control. Just as in birth, we must allow ourselves to be broken. We must die to our identities as mothers. We must allow ourselves to be transformed all over again; the process turns our lives to shades of black and blue—but the healing rays of rest and release wait for us. When we turn from the hurtful shadows, we step into the Sabbath's light.

CHAPTER FIVE

Juggling Act

"Confidante, personal advisor, lover, referee, peacemaker, housekeeper, laundress, chauffeur, interior decorator, gardener, painter, wallpaperer, veterinarian, manicurist, barber, seamstress, appointment manager, bookkeeper,...teacher, disciplinarian, entertainer, psychoanalyst, nurse,...dietician and nutritionist, baker, chef...." According to Ann Landers' 1988 column, these are only a few of women's roles. What is more, this list is confined to the job titles that fall under the general heading of wife and mother. Most women also juggle several other identities: employee, daughter, church member, community volunteer, friend, neighbor. No wonder we sometimes feel like frantic jugglers, tossing the spinning plates higher and higher, faster and faster, trying desperately not to let them smash around us on the floor.

Not only are we juggling responsibilities, we're also juggling our attitudes about life. We must tie our lives to our children's. We must let them go. We must die to self. We must defend our own identities. Our lives are filled with paradox.

A University of Michigan study ("Juggling Contradictions: Women's Ideas About Families"[46]) found that the women who participated in the research all managed to combine two contradictory belief systems, what the study calls the "familiar" and the "individualistic." The familial belief system affirms that the needs of the family are paramount; they come first no matter what. Meanwhile, the individualistic point of view acknowledges a mother's own personal needs as being equal in importance to the family's needs. We have the right to our own careers, our own friends, our own leisure activities, our own separate fulfillment. How do we resolve the conflict between these two belief systems? Can we resolve them? Or do we as modern mothers toss these contradictions back and forth, like potatoes too hot for us to grab and hold?

Juggling as fast as we can, we still can't help dropping one or two (or sometimes all) of those spinning plates. They roll away into the shadows and we scramble to pick them up, to regain our rhythm. But with our hands so full, how can God expect us to have time for spirituality?

Shadow: Frustration

But you ask too much, I want to cry out.
I cannot be having a baby and be a good housekeeper
and keep thinking...and be always free to...give to the children
...and keep my mind clear and open.... I cannot.
Anne Morrow Lindbergh [47]

I never seem able to meet all my responsibilities at the same time. If I teach a class at church, then weeks go by when I fail to spend time with an elderly neighbor. If I spend "quality time" with my kids, then my laundry pile mounts higher and higher. If my writing is going well, then too many suppers consist of take-out pizza or warmed-up leftovers. While I talk to a friend over coffee, dust collects on the surfaces of my house, and although I've managed to be on time for morning appointments every day this week, I'm afraid I haven't made my bed once. I feel guilty and inept, pulled between my conflicting responsibilities. Like many mothers, I can't possibly catch all the spinning pieces of my life, and yet all of us want so much to be able to do everything well. (*After all,* whispers our hearts, *if you were a Good Mother you could do it all.*) When we're not successful, frustration casts a dismal shade across our lives.

We may not be surprised that Anne Morrow Lindbergh, the writer, mother, and wife of the famous aviator, had these same feelings—but Saint Teresa? Surely not the doctor of the church, the author of *The Interior Castle*, a celibate, spiritual woman who devoted her life to contemplation and the interior life. And yet she wrote, "I am always stealing the time for writing and that with great difficulty for it hinders me from spinning and I...have numerous other things to do."[48] Like us, she understood that stopping the relentless juggle of responsibilities is not easy. When we do take a moment to pray, our minds still automatically continue the frantic tossing of worries and daydreams.

But as mothers we are not alone in our predicament. "Many people," writes Evelyn Underhill,

> greatly desiring the life of communion with God, find no opportunity for attention to Him in an existence which often lacks privacy and is conditioned by ceaseless household duties, exacting professional responsibilities or long hours of work. The great spiritual teachers, who are not nearly so aloof from normal life as those who do not read them suppose, have often dealt with this situation.[49]

Spiritual women down through the ages have struggled to juggle the pieces of their lives, just as we do. Catherine of Genoa snatched at whirling balls of spiritual ecstasy in between the dull ordinariness of hospital housekeeping and accounts. Elizabeth Fry grasped her devotion to God even while she reached to toss and catch the flashing knives of Newgate Prison's filth and danger. Elizabeth Leseur flung her physical energy into housekeeping, tossed high the torch of her husband's emotional abuse, and managed to catch the spiritual truths she recorded in her journal, truths that spun so bright they changed her husband's life after her death. And Susanna Wesley, the mother of the founder of Methodism, wrote, "O God, I find it most difficult to preserve a devout and serious temper in the midst of much worldly business.... I would... that I had more leisure to retire from the world without injuring those dependent on me."[50] Like us, all these women were jugglers.

Nor are the frustrations of juggling unique to us as women. Saint Cuthbert and Thomas Merton both longed for the solitude and freedom of a hermitage. Both men instead juggled their spirituality with the busy give-and-take of community life. Saints Ambrose and Augustine snatched at spiritual truths while keeping aloft a bishop's hectic duties.

Saint Francis Xavier would have preferred to remain in stillness at the feet of Saint Ignatius, and Henry Martyn was an English intellectual who would have gladly spent his whole life in quiet meditation. Instead they were both sent out as missionaries and spent their energy stretching to catch all the many responsibilities of active service.

A pattern is emerging here. From our human viewpoint, we think we'd do so much better if we had just one apple to toss slowly and carefully, up and down, up and down, catching it perfectly each time. Maybe we could handle two apples, or even an orange along with the apples—but not this impossible rushing cycle of apples, oranges, bananas, rubber balls, spinning plates, burning torches, flashing knives. Life asks too much of us, and failure is inevitable. And yet for some reason, God often requires of us this dark frustration.

Like the other saints and like us, Teresa of Avila understood frustration. She was no hermit who devoted her life to God in silence and solitude. All the while she was writing *The Interior Castle*, all the while she was racing along her spiritual path (and creeping and staggering and crawling), she was at the same time immersed in church politics and the busy life of a community. Like us, she was often cross, often exhausted, often even desperate. She knew she was falling short of God's ideal, that the spinning plates were crashing on her head, out of control, and that the most important plate of all, her spirituality, was collecting dust in the corner—and yet, with all her struggles, with all her failures, God's grace pulled her forward.

God allows few of us the constantly smooth and quiet existence we think we crave—but maybe that's because the Divine One knows the pride we'd take if we could accomplish our spiritual growth all by ourselves, with our own careful effort. Whenever we fail, when the pieces of our lives drop from our hands and bounce off into the corners, we rage against our loss of control like thwarted two-year-olds. And once again, we are forced to surrender our selfish egos that long to rule the world. Once again, we can rely only on grace.

Grace is not something that depends on our own success and competence. Instead, it is the magnet that pulls our spinning, fragmented lives forward, toward their goal. Surrounded by the shadows of our frustration, God's grace gleams brighter than gold.

He did not say, "You shall not be tempest-tossed,
you shall not be work-weary, you shall not be discomforted...
But he said, "You shall not be overcome."
Julian of Norwich [51]

Sunshine: Unified Vision and Holy Play

The time of business
does not with me differ from the time of prayer;
and in the noise and clatter of my kitchen,
while several persons are at the same time calling for different
things, I possess God in as great tranquility as if I were on my knees.
Brother Lawrence [52]

As I began working on this chapter, the metaphor of juggling seemed to epitomize the frustration I often feel with my life. I couldn't imagine what could be the sunshine of a mother's juggling act. As I researched the actual art of juggling, however. I found that the metaphor offers us hope.

Juggling, says juggler Steve Cohen, "takes many elements and creates a cohesive, unified, manageable system." It requires "perseverance forged of thoughtful choices pieced together to establish a new unity."[53] In other words, as mothers juggling the contradictory pieces of our identities, we too can create lives that are nevertheless whole and unified. Turning back to an earlier metaphor, we, like the Amish quilters, seem to be working only with tiny, individual pieces of fabric. In reality, however, each piece is held together by its common purpose, for we are stitching a life united by a guiding vision. Juggling provides us with another image that empowers us to make this possible. Our spirituality is not, after all, just one more spinning plate we have to try to keep up in the air with all the others. Instead, it can be the thing that unifies the many elements of our life into a manageable whole.

When Thérèse of Lisieux first began her spiritual journey, she was, like many of us, obsessed with exterior perfection. Gradually, though, she let go of her need for outward success. Then, she wrote, "my only guide is self-abandonment. I have no other compass." She goes on to describe this as "the complete abandonment of a baby sleeping without fear."[54] This peaceful and confident commitment to God can unify our identities.

Abandonment to God will never be the guiding force in our lives, however, as long as our work is ego-centered, our achievement a form of self-gratification. Brother Lawrence, the seventeenth-century writer of *The Practice of the Presence of God*, wrote "Our sanctification does not depend on our changing our work, but in doing that for God's sake, which we commonly do for our own." [55] Saint Paul the Apostle said that whatever we do, we should do for the glory of God

(1 Cor. 10:31). This is our call, the vocation that gives a cohesive meaning to the contradictory segments of our lives. When this God-oriented perspective infuses our lives, it gives us an identity that is constant, despite our changing external roles.

What's more, it brings together our conflicting attitudes, for we do not serve self at the cost of our children, or our children at the cost of self. Many self-help authors write today of the inner child, and as mothers, all of us have a little girl who lives forever inside us, a little girl who is sometimes hurt, sometimes delighted, often frustrated, occasionally frightened. God, our Good Mother, loves this little girl as much as the other children in our families—and sometimes I find that when I think of my inner child as just one more member of the family, then I am freed from the up-and-down toss of guilt and resentment. Treating each child fairly in our families is not always easy, but we do not insist that one child always sacrifice her desires to the rest, nor do we expect another to be always satisfied at the cost of the others. God asks that we strive to treat our own inner child with the same equality. As we offer our lives to God, both self and family are affirmed within the Divine.

According to Evelyn Underhill, the saints were able to achieve this cohesive sense of vocation because they understood "that what is asked of us is not necessarily a great deal of time devoted to what we regard as spiritual things, but the constant offering of our wills to God, so that the practical duties which fill most of our days can become part of [Divine] order and be given spiritual worth."[56] Like Saint Thérèse, abandonment alone must guide us. We must let go of our need for control. We must simply trust, releasing the spinning particles of our lives one by one into God's hand. A juggler, says Cohen, learns this art "one manageable, chaos-free step at a time."[57]

This is essential for juggling, for although good jugglers create a new unity out of many elements, they focus on only one ball at time. However, if their focus were to *stay* on one ball, all the others would drop. In other words, as jugglers we must learn to let go *fast*, shifting our focus to the next thing life asks of us as though it were the only thing that mattered, releasing our lives into God's will. We get in trouble only when we won't let go of the last ball—or when we turn our attention ahead to the one that's still up in the air.

Says Cohen,

As the balls begin to fly away, you will instinctively try to pick them up. Turning this way and that, lunging, reaching, grabbing forward and back at the bounding spheres, you may find yourself dizzyingly lurching in more directions than you ever thought existed.[58]

The only way to avoid this dizzy, lurching existence is to live in the present moment, without looking backward or forward. Only in the present, in the fleeting *now*, do time and eternity intersect. Only here do we find Shekinah's immediacy: the reality of the God who uses the name I AM (Ex 3:14). Our sense of frustration comes when we look back at what we failed to do and forward to what still needs to be done. If, instead, we concentrate only on the job at hand, releasing it at once when the time comes to move on to our next responsibility, then we are saying yes to the present moment—and we are free to find God there.

This freedom gives our lives a new lightness, takes away some of the overwhelming weight of our responsibilities. After all, the word *juggle* comes from the Latin for *to jest or joke*, and as God's jugglers we are freed from some of the grown-up world's heavy seriousness. We are free to play. Evelyn Underhill writes,

> The action of those whose lives are given to the Spirit
> has in it something of the leisure of Eternity, and be-
> cause of this, they achieve far more than those whose

lives are enslaved by the rush and hurry, the unceasing tick-tick of the world. In the spiritual life it is very important to get our timing right. Otherwise we tend to forget that God...is greater than the job.[59]

The ancient Greeks spoke of two different kinds of time: *chronos*, clock time, and *kairos*, the eternal now. We inhabit both kinds of time, but too often the "tick-tick" of *chronos* whispers annoyingly in our ears no matter what we're doing, distracting our attention from the playful leisure of *kairos*—and those are the times when we lose our timing and begin to drop the whirling pieces of our lives.

The Shakers, an American religious community that created beautiful, symmetrical furniture and architecture, had this phrase as their motto: "Hearts to God, hands to work." When our inner selves are focused on God, then like the Shakers, our outward physical actions will transform our inner vision into concrete reality.

The contemplative life and the life of action are not in opposition as we have so often supposed. Instead, contemplation can be embedded in the heart of action. The word *contemplation* can be broken down into two parts: *con* meaning *with*, and *templation* meaning a sacred measure, a vision of divine time. In his book *Gratefulness, the Heart of Prayer*, Brother David Steindl-Rast puts together these two pieces of the word and concludes that contemplation truly means "action plus vision."[60]

This does not mean that we must somehow have spiritual thoughts occupying our minds even while we are immersed in changing diapers, washing clothes, or cooking supper. Instead, says Steindl-Rast, our actions themselves can be contemplation, a way of coming to know God's love from within by acting it out. In other words, the business of our lives can somehow be sacramental. Even scrubbing toilets can reveal the divine.

"But what if I'm not even thinking of God?" Steindl-Rast writes. "Can this still be prayer?"

> Well, are you still breathing, even though you are not thinking of the breath you breathe? Action is realized by action, not by thinking about it. And contemplation in action is that contemplation in which we realize God by acting in love. Thinking about God is important. But acting in God leads to a deeper knowledge. Lovers are closer to love than scholars who merely reflect on love.[61]

The single-minded attention that our many roles require of us can in itself be prayer, for almost all of our roles as mothers ask that we put our love into action. "Prayer," wrote John Wesley, "continues in the desire of the heart though the understanding be employed on outward things. In souls filled with love, the desire to please God is a continual prayer."[62]

As mothers, our selfishness has been cracked open by our many responsibilities to others. We try to catch all the broken, juggled pieces of our identity, but too often we fail. When our spiritual vision is united with our physical action, however, somehow our busy, fragmented lives turn into prayer and contemplation. This requires obedience on our part, a simple obedience to the requirements of any given moment. But as Saint Teresa says, "If contemplation,...prayer, nursing the sick, the work of the house and the most menial labour, all serve this Guest, why should we choose to minister to him in one way rather than another?"[63] In God's eyes, each moment, each responsibility is equally sacred, equally significant, so long as in the midst of our work we are contemplating God rather than ourselves.

The contemplative life, for all its freedom and playfulness, for all its significance and joy, does not come easily or naturally to us. It requires a radical readjustment of the way we look at our lives, and we cannot achieve this new attitude merely by reading over this chapter or by longing for it to be true. "Nothing is as easy as that," says Evelyn Underhill.

> It means discipline of thought and of feeling, a more careful use of such leisure as we have; and filling our minds with ideas that point the right way instead of suggestions which distract us from God and spiritual things. It must also mean some time, even though this may be very short time, given and given definitely, to communion with Him.... We must use even the few minutes that we have in this way, and let the spirit of these few minutes spread throughout the busy hours.... Unless we are prepared to make this the centre of our life...we need not hope for results.[64]

We long for results, but trying something new means taking a risk. It means we will not automatically succeed at first, that instead we are bound to fail. Sometimes frustration's shadow seems more comfortable than learning to really juggle. After all, we're familiar with these shadows; they're safe, for they ask no new effort of us.

As Underhill said, no effort comes easily. It will almost certainly require that we nudge ourselves awake occasionally. Bells are the ancient reminder to call us to prayer. A friend of mine finds her oven timer works just as well, though for me its buzz would echo with *chronos'* irritating insistence. I'm looking instead for repeating patterns in my life that will help keep me alert. For instance, phrases my children say, actions that I do (like cleaning something), or little pauses as simple as sitting at a red light or waiting for my computer to boot up. Another woman I know whispers, "Your mercies endure forever," whenever she sees the color purple. Whatever small specific thing works for each of us, it can call our hearts to attention. After all, this juggling act we perform is a game we play, and its fun can infuse our lives with significance.

The busier we are, though, the more we need our eyes focused on that which is the center of our lives, the unifying vision. Our lives need a basic order, a discipline that will structure all the frantic pieces. "Find someone who can juggle five of anything," says Cohen, "and watch the quickness, agile dexterity, and focused strength it takes to be a silly juggler."[65] Only within discipline's framework do we have room to play.

We become adept at doing more than one thing at once. For some of us this means talking on a portable phone while we do laundry, praying while we drive, grabbing whatever time we can. Different things work for different people. Dorothy Day, the founder of the Catholic Worker Movement, wrote,

> Because I am a woman involved in practical cares, I cannot give the first half of the day to these things, but must meditate when I can, early in the morning, on the fly during the day. Not in privacy...but here, there, and everywhere—at the kitchen table...on my way to and from appointments and even while making supper or putting [my daughter] to bed.[66]

Nevertheless, every juggler drops things sometimes. Everyone gets frustrated, for obviously this is not a skill we were born with. Brother Lawrence was also not born knowing how to practice the presence of God. Instead, he wrote that he needed ten years of failed effort before he could begin to experience success. We must be patient with ourselves.

Juggling, says Steve Cohen, "like any goal, happens in time," and it requires "toleration and persistence. Free from anxiety about wild success or dismal failure, your determination to be as simply conscious as you can be, can make it all come together.... After a drop, all you need to do is pick up the balls and start throwing again."[67] And sometimes we need to be realistic enough to know when we must choose to let something drop. We are not God; we cannot do everything at once.

But we do not juggle alone. Whether we know it or not, this is a game God plays with us.

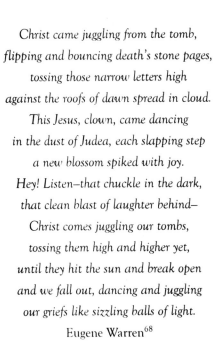

Christ came juggling from the tomb,
flipping and bouncing death's stone pages,
tossing those narrow letters high
against the roofs of dawn spread in cloud.
This Jesus, clown, came dancing
in the dust of Judea, each slapping step
a new blossom spiked with joy.
Hey! Listen—that chuckle in the dark,
that clean blast of laughter behind—
Christ comes juggling our tombs,
tossing them high and higher yet,
until they hit the sun and break open
and we fall out, dancing and juggling
our griefs like sizzling balls of light.
Eugene Warren[68]

When we were children, we knew both limitation's frustration and play's joyful single-mindedness. Now, as mothers, the juggle of our lives calls us to experience again this pattern of sunshine and shadow. We cannot control all the factors of our lives; we can only toss the busy pieces up into God's waiting hands. Some days the Divine Juggler seems to drop us, but what falls out "like sizzling balls of light" are only our selfishness and sorrow. And we learn to not take ourselves too seriously, for in the midst of our frustration we hear the echo of holy laughter.

CHAPTER SIX

Housework

As mothers, one of the heaviest balls we juggle is that of housework. Nothing (except our culture's tradition) says that mothers should be solely responsible for the work of the house; fathers and children are equally capable of picking up this unwieldy ball. A University of Michigan study found, however, that in half the families who participated, the mothers did all the housework. In the other half men "helped," but women remained primarily responsible.[69] As men's and women's roles become more equal, men will most likely take on more and more responsibility for housework, but even then women will undoubtedly still be responsible for at least half of the home's work.

A generation or two ago, our culture tended to romanticize this work. Keeping house was the ultimate goal of all little girls. The endless cycle of cooking and cleaning, washing and mending would bring all women to completion and fulfillment. Even today, many television commercials would have us believe that we will be serene and smiling mothers so long as we have the right cleaning products available. Our children, dressed in their perfectly laundered clothes, will dance joyfully through green meadows. We will smile widely at our gleaming kitchen floors and we will laugh tolerantly with other mothers despite spills and mishaps—all because our cleaning closet is well stocked. And if frustration and despair do enter our hearts, they will quickly be chased away when we switch to a better, more efficient detergent or toilet cleaner.

The truth is, though, few of us love housework. It's sheer drudgery, after all, an endless, thankless job that no one notices until we fail to do it. Most of us have better things to do.

And yet despite housework's monotony, God's saints (even the male saints) have found that this work too can be a holy service, a service not only to our families but also to God.

Shadow: Repetitive Monotony

Remember that someone must cook the meals....
Reflect that true humility consists in being willing and ready
to do what our Lord asks of us.
Teresa of Avila[70]

I don't like housework. And I don't like having to tidy up the same room tonight that I did this morning and that I will again tomorrow. I don't like the fact that the kitchen should be cleaned three times a day. I don't like the never-ending mound of dirty clothes that tumbles down my laundry chute. And I don't like having to quit writing every afternoon so I can think of something to cook for supper. Someone has to keep the house clean and wash the clothes and cook the meals—but I wish it didn't have to be me.

Sometimes, as mothers, we feel like the family servants, the nearly invisible presences who quietly transform chaos back into order. We have so many more important, more creative things to do, and yet hours and hours of our lives are spent vacuuming the same floors, washing the same clothes, scrubbing the same bathtubs—and no one even notices or thanks us.

By function, we often *are* servants. Unfortunately, we have enough of our great-grandparents' prejudices that we connect servanthood with being third-class citizens. After all, who but the underclass would agree to do such monotonous work? No wonder then that housework's endless tedium sometimes fills us with resentment.

The Bible has a very different way of looking at service, however, for service is at Christianity's heart. Christ, creation's

King, came "not to be served but to serve" (Mt 20:25-28). When he washed his disciples' feet he modeled the sort of service that selfless love demands. He showed us that service by its very nature involves the ordinary, the trivial, the monotonous.

Thérèse of Lisieux based her "Little Way" to holiness on these same small drudgeries that we experience as mothers. Hers was a ministry of trifles, a series of minuscule deaths to self, each one rising out of the everyday tedium of service.

The Rule of Saint Benedict is another spiritual path that has much in common with our lives as mothers. The Rule speaks of various sorts of work: ordinary manual labor, intellectual labor (reading and scholarly study), and creative labor (the work of artisans), and it then concludes that one form of work is not more valuable than another, for all can be part of the community's foundation which is the Work of God. (In other words, the Benedictines are good jugglers, for they have a cohesive vision to unify their separate responsibilities.)

Speaking of Saint Benedict's Rule, Brian C. Taylor says,

To become fully human in this life as it has been given to us is to allow the sacredness of the ordinary to become manifest. To see God in work, cooking, prayer, community,...and dealing with possessions is to enter into the mystery of the incarnation.[71]

Even in our ordinary chores, Christ's reality can be revealed. Thomas Merton speaks of "an unspeakable reverence for the holiness of created things,"[72] a reverence that makes even dirty dishes and muddy floors sacramental. When we learn to treat housework's tedium with this unspoken reverence, then perhaps we will be surprised to discover that God's presence is found in our everyday routines even more meaningfully than in our lives' heroic crises and spectacular achievements.

In an article on Saint Benedict's Rule, Cistercian monk Michael Casey speaks of "creative monotony."[73] Monotony grounds us: it commits us to the here and now and forces us to stop running here and there looking for distraction and gratification. Routine gives us stability and focus; it helps us order life's chaos and it channels our being into paths of holiness.

What is more, routine's strong framework, even its tedious repetition, can send reflections of God's constancy into our bored gloom. We make a bed, it is unmade that night, and we remake it in the morning. We dust the furniture; after a few days, the furniture is once more dusty, and we dust it again. We do the laundry, we do the laundry, we do the laundry. This work that has to be done over and over and over reflects the natural and spiritual cycles of growth and loss, birth and death, and most of all God's unceasing redemption.

Still, we're only human—it's hard not to get frustrated; we're used to thinking of work as a concrete symbol of our personal achievement and success. No wonder we're angry when dirty footprints are tracked across our new-mopped floor, or when the room we just cleaned is once more full of toys. "How would you feel," I always ask my husband, "if you had just finished a report at work, had it all neatly typed and stapled, and the children came in and scribbled on some pages, then ripped the others into shreds? Would you just smile patiently and start all over?" Of course he wouldn't. I'm afraid when my hard work is undone again and again, I seldom smile either.

That's because my ego is invested in my work. If we're to escape the inevitable frustration and anger that lurks in the darkness of our daily chores, then we need to relinquish our achievement orientation. Housework's repetition offers us a chance to step away from our goal-oriented outlook, our thirst for success. If we let go of our need to make progress, and instead are willing to make no progress, we agree to inhabit monotony's shadows, confident that grace will reach us even here.

Elizabeth Goudge in her novel *Green Dolphin Country* describes a mother who is unable to pray after the death of her children:

> But she found, as she bent to her scrubbing, that she had left the pain of that terrible memory behind her.... Perhaps the Holy Mother had taken it from her and would use it instead of prayer. The Holy Mother had been a good housewife in her day, and doubtless knew how to make use of all the bits and pieces that came to hand.[74]

Sometimes the mindlessness of housework serves as a deeper prayer than any that employs our intellect. Like us, like Mary, God makes use of all the "bits and pieces" of our lives.

What's more, housework's dark side disciplines our selfishness. Eventually, after years of practice, it may even transform our ego-love into humility. The Lamb of God's lowliness and meekness will be reflected in our lives.

But this meek humility is not the Milquetoast, doormat variety. Service is at the center of Christianity, but so, too, is freedom of choice. Christ does not call us to be slaves, who submit to someone else's demands. Instead, we are asked to pick up service voluntarily, with our own free will. In pregnancy we learned to open ourselves; now we can choose to open ourselves to housework's tedium. We embrace it voluntarily so that both we and it can be transformed.

This responsibility does not belong to us mothers alone, however. During the Middle Ages, a time when society was ruled by hierarchy, the religious community was a sign to the world of God's grace, for monasteries and convents were societies based on equality. In religious communities, everyone undertakes the daily work together. All are equal. The same can be true in our families. As we learn to see housework's monotony as a vehicle of love and growth, our families can also become signs to the world. They can demonstrate that God does not divide us into ranking categories. Instead, through Christ's redemption, we are "neither slave nor free, male nor female" (Gal 3:28). The endless work of the house belongs to us all.

We ought not to be weary
of doing little things for the love of God,
who regards not the greatness of the work,
but the love with which it is performed.
We should not wonder if, in the beginning,
we often failed in our endeavors,

but that at last we should gain a habit,
which will naturally produce its acts in us, without our care.
Brother Lawrence[75]

Sunshine: Holy Service

The...service that one should perform for another in a Christian community is that of active helpfulness. This means, initially, simple assistance in trifling, external matters. There is a magnitude of these things wherever people live together.... One who worries about the loss of time that such petty, outward acts of helpfulness entail is usually taking the importance if his own career too solemnly.

Dietrich Bonhoeffer[76]

Our families are small communities, and within them we do, as Bonhoeffer says, experience a "magnitude" of opportunities for service. We are accustomed to thinking of Christian service in terms that are nobler, more dramatic, more like Mother Teresa in the slums of Calcutta or Florence Nightingale on the battlefields of the Crimea, but even for women like Mother

Teresa and Florence Nightingale, service boils down to "simple assistance in trifling, external matters." For us, as mothers, this means things as trivial as matching socks, packing lunches, or wiping kitchen tables. "Be faithful in little things," Mother Teresa advises, "for in them our strength lies."[77]

These small services must be directed outward if they are to crack open our selfishness. Self-righteous, self-centered service demands visible, external rewards, but the sort of service that Jesus modeled does not concern itself with results. Instead, it is contented even with obscurity.

Jeremy Taylor's *Rule and Exercises of Holy Living*, written in the seventeenth century, says that we should "love to be concealed, and little esteemed; be content to lack praise, never be troubled when thou art slighted or undervalued."[78] This way of thinking is alien to us today, however; we're so accustomed to finding our value in the rewards of our work. We resent being undervalued.

As women being transformed by motherhood's disciplines, we need to remind ourselves that our value springs from God's love. We find our truest identities in the midst of unmerited grace. "If you are humble," says Mother Teresa, "nothing will touch you, neither praise nor disgrace, because you know what you are."[79] We too can know who we are; we are not simply drudges, toiling endlessly; we are creators who are constructing a home for our own small community.

For some of us, this type of thinking comes easier than for others. A few of my friends have a true knack for home-making. Although they may not like all aspects of housework, they receive satisfaction and fulfillment from creating homes that are warm and comfortable and lovely. As for me, I like a home that's clean and cozy as much as anyone, but the process of keeping it that way is a constant challenge to me, a challenge that all too often tips me backward into the shadows, from holy service into monotony.

I like to remind myself, though, of the artisans who built the great cathedrals of the Middle Ages. They carved the back sides of statues as carefully as they did the fronts, for they did not have our attitude that only what is noticed and appreciated is worth our effort. They inscribed intricate designs on stones that were hidden by doors, perched gargoyles on walls too high for anyone to see, and even painted pictures on the undersides of seats. Their achievement was not ego-centered, like ours so often is today, dependent on external affirmation. Instead, their work was offered up to God's glory.

Christians today, though, tend to disparage physical appearances. We feel guilty for wanting our private homes to be beautiful, for surely this beauty, benefiting no one but ourselves, would be worldly or selfish. True, our society is obsessed with appearances, and we do not want to make possessions too important or forget those who have so much less. But in the process, we have sometimes thrown out the baby with the bath water. We have divorced God from our homes.

The Divine is revealed intimately within our families. Consequently, our homes are sacred places. They should speak to us of God just as clearly as our churches do. Judaism is more apt to remember the home's holiness, but too often Christians have forgotten. We relegate God to our churches, forgetting that most of Christ's ministry, including the Last Supper, took place in private homes.

Just as in Christ's day, our homes are meant to be welcoming places, places of security and grace that reflect God's nature. "Lord, you have been our dwelling place," says Psalm 90:1. If we remember that our houses are Divine metaphors, then housework takes on a whole new significance.

I will let no tiny sacrifice pass....
I wish to profit by the smallest actions and to do them for love.
Thérèse of Lisieux[80]

Alchemy was the process medieval scientists believed would transform *prima materia*, ordinary dull metal, into gold. As mothers, we use prayer and love to transform our ordinary housework into something that shines on our lives' dullness. Our routine chores are the *prima materia* that are changed into holy service; we grow spiritually by means of everyday work. In the midst of folding laundry or scrubbing a bathtub, remember: we are God's alchemists, changing drudgery to gold.

CHAPTER SEVEN

Failure

We enter motherhood with the highest of hopes. We imagine the joy, the laughter, the fulfillment—but we don't imagine all the ways we ourselves will fail to live up to our bright fantasies. Our mother-love is sewn tight to our identities, and yet, over and over, we find that we fail our children. That failure rips at the seams of our self-images. It shreds our false security and tumbles us out naked into despair's gray shade.

In no other relationship do we expect perfection of ourselves. With our children, though, we want to be Good Mothers—and Good Mothers are perfect. They are always patient, always wise. They keep their children healthy and happy and safe. When we fail to do any of these Good Mother duties, then a terrible blow is struck to our sense of who we are.

Our feelings of failure come in all shapes and sizes, and at any point on motherhood's long path. We may feel we are failures because we were unable to give birth and were forced to adopt our children. We may think we have failed if we had a C-section or if we resorted to some other medical intervention rather than giving birth naturally. We may not take to breast-feeding the way we imagined we would, and that too feels like failure. We blame ourselves if our children have some physical or intellectual quality that makes them different from other children. We feel at fault if they are seriously sick. If, as teenagers and young adults, they fail to conform to what we think is good for them, then again we blame ourselves. This sense of our imperfection can be a niggling insecurity at the back of our minds, rising from something as trivial as our daily failure to be patient, or it can be a hopeless depression caused by that greatest of all our fears, the greatest of all our perceived failures: a child's death. But whether our failure is profound or commonplace, any time we don't measure up to the Good Mother's perfection we experience our own inadequacy.

The darkness is overwhelming. The only way we know to escape it is to try even harder to achieve perfection. Sooner or later, though, we face the truth: our own strength is not enough. Blind, hopeless, we eventually come to accept the dark. And when God finds us, we understand at last that grace is independent of any effort of our own.

Poet Wendell Berry says,

> To go in the dark with a light is to know the light.
> To know the dark, go dark. Go without sight,
> and find that the dark, too, blooms and sings,
> and is traveled by dark feet and dark wings.[81]

Shadow: Confronting Our Own Inadequacy

I fail, I fail, I fail—I could say it a thousand times....
How many imperfections I see in myself!
I would like to be knocked unconscious
so that I am no longer aware of my wickedness.
Lord, knock grace into me.
Teresa of Avila[82]

I was a very smug new mother. As a baby, my oldest daughter was happy and healthy and easily pleased. She ate well, laughed often, and best of all, she soon slept through the night and dependably took long naps. She was the perfect little companion, and mothering her filled me with delight.

With a sense of wondering pity, I watched other mothers who were frazzled and frustrated. I could not imagine ever being impatient with my daughter. I could not imagine that I would ever be anything but a Good Mother. And then my second child was born.

My son was a very different sort of baby. He went straight from colic to chronic ear infections, and he cried endlessly. My sweet, compliant daughter, angry and hurt by the changes in her world, saw how quickly her parents responded to the baby's screaming, and she began to scream too, the smallest frustration sending her into a storm of shrieking rage. As for me, the serene and satisfied Good Mother who had never been anything but patient and tender—well, to my horror, I found myself screaming too.

These were dark days for me. I was exhausted by caring for my son, drained by my inability to stop his crying. I would put on earphones and listen to loud, happy music so I could hold him without hearing his constant cries, so I would not give in to the terrible, black urge to shake him until he was quiet. Hiding my anger from my daughter, though, was harder, especially when she kicked and wailed and refused to learn to use the toilet. I wanted her to be the way she had been before the baby was born, just as she wanted the same from me. Like her, I was angry and frustrated and hurt that I was no longer in control of my world. Worst of all, I knew I was not a Good Mother after all. I was a failure.

Blessed Concepción Cabrera de Armida, a wife and the mother of nine children, understood these dark moments that happen to all mothers. She wrote, "I have wasted the better part of my life in vanities, in imaginations, in vain pleasures and in foolish illusions.... There are immense voids in my life: I have not always done my duty to...the members of my family.... Instead of seeking God, I have sought myself."[83]

She also understood that when we insist on the Good Mother's perfection, then we are not seeking God but ourselves and we are doomed to failure. "If I cling to human affection I shall find nothing but illusion and disappointment," she wrote. "Do You in mercy tear me away from all that is not Yourself."[84]

When we experience failure in our motherhood, then we are not being torn from our children, but from our own egos, from the self-centered identities we have clung to all our lives. What an ego trip it would be to lift our children with our strength and competence, high above disappointment and anger, sickness and harm—and how it hurts both our love and our pride when we can't.

We are mortals living in an uncertain world and we cannot protect our children from all the risks the world holds. What is more, hurt and frustration are givens in the mother-child dyad, just as they are in any human relationship. No matter how much we love each other, sooner or later we all hurt one another.

As our children grow older, they become adept at pointing out our failures to us, making a list of any that might have escaped our attention. Facing our failure hurts. But the truth is we have failed them, and we must release them from our own yearning to be stroked and affirmed. We are not Perfect Mothers, no matter how much we want to be. Admitting our imperfections is humbling, but our children need to know we are not God. Out of a mixture of motives, both selfish and loving, we would like to be—but we aren't.

Even the saints experienced this most intimate failure. Elizabeth Seton wrote in her journal,

The heart down-discouraged at the constant failure of good resolutions—so soon disturbed by trifles—so little interior recollection...the reproaches of disobedience to the little ones much more applicable to myself.[85]

We all fail our children, just as our parents all failed us, just as our children will one day fail their children. The experience is an age-old cycle. We'd like to be immune from the wheel of pain. We'd like to think we know more than our own mothers did or that we love our children more or that our level of understanding is somehow greater, that for whatever reason we won't make the same mistakes our mothers did. But we will. In one way or another, we wound our children.

If we didn't, though, if we were the Perfect Mothers we long to be, ever-loving and ever-nourishing, then our children would never separate from us. They would remain needy and dependent, rather than growing into strong and whole individuals. And they would never realize their own need for God, for something bigger and beyond themselves. In God's paradoxical economy, hurt brings health. By Christ's "wounds we are healed" (Is 53:5), and even our own wounds, despite their pain, are put to use. Not that we should be sadists, hurting our children "for their own good," but our mistakes can be infused with God's creative grace.

For God is creating not only our children's identities, but our own as well. Just as our children must separate from us in order to be both whole and holy, so must we separate our self-worth from them. Here again, in failure's bleakest of all shadows, we continue to learn to let go of our children, to allow them to be separate from ourselves. If we do not, we not only hurt them, but we also will not be true to ourselves, to the complete selves God has called us to be.

George MacDonald, the nineteenth-century clergyman who wrote *The Princess and the Goblins* and other children's fantasies, says that God has given each one of us a name which "no one knoweth saving [the one] that receiveth it." We each have our individual relationship to God, and, says MacDonald, we each can say, God "has called me that which I like best."[86] God delights in us mothers too, not just in our children. The Divine One forgives us and heals us and surrounds us with love. Our worth does not depend on our success as mothers, nor does it depend on our children's behavior or achievement. Our worth is buried in our own secret communion with God. No matter how hard we try, we cannot be perfect, but that is irrelevant to our identities. The Good Mother's image is a fantasy; God does not call us by her name.

As human beings, however, we tend to feel safer in a world that is categorized, all neatly labeled *good* and *bad, success* and *failure*. If we could, we'd stuff God into one of our tidy pigeonholes, and then we'd feel more in control. Over and over again, though, God smashes our neat compartments, reminding us that the Divine is far bigger than any category we imagine. God uses even our failures to break free of our preconceptions.

Like us, the saints had to let go of their own images of what was good. Jane de Chantal, a seventeenth-century mother and widow, felt called to found a community of women who would give their lives to actively helping the poor. The religious hierarchy of the day would not allow the women to leave their convents, though, and Jane was forced to accept that her communities would remain separate from the world, even while they devoted their lives to praying for it. She must have felt she had failed. Clare of Assisi longed to see her beloved friend Francis once more before he died. Instead, she was too sick to go to him when he was dying, and she could only gaze at his already dead face through her window's iron grill. She must have felt as though her love were a failure. Saint Joan of Arc, when she was first brought to the stake, denied her visions and faith, so terrified was she of the fire. The next time she was braver, but obviously, she did not see being burned at the stake as what she would have chosen as her life's crowning achievement. By human standards, her life had failed. And Teresa of Avila, for all her intelligence and mystic maturity, died while the order she had founded was being torn apart by divisiveness, a failure that must have hurt her terribly. Somehow, though, Divine creativity turned all their failures to triumph—just as we see in Christ's life and death. After all, Jesus had only three years of ministry before the political powers put him to death. Surely the crucifixion could have seemed the greatest failure of all.

Author Robert Farrar Capon says that Christ's followers deliberately celebrate the worst thing the human race has ever done: the murder of God Incarnate. "They haven't run away from the evil," he writes, "they've actually made it the centerpiece of their celebration. They've taken what should have caused only alienation, and, by the pardon that flows from it to them, they've turned it into a festival of reconciliation."[87] The crucifixion was our failure as well as God's, yet in the midst of this failure—not in spite of it, but because of it—we achieve our true identities. This sort of contradiction is at Christianity's heart. Apparently God loves a good paradox, maybe to keep us from getting too pat in our thinking. All our analysis and theology go only so far...and then there's simply Mystery.

At any rate, our success in God's time, in *kairos*, is not measured by our accomplishment in *chronos*. We're so used to living in *chronos* time that we forget God transcends it. The crucifixion, the worst of all failures, became the means for our healing, and God can transform our own failures into triumphs of redemption and grace.

But this won't happen until we let go of our images of perfection. Our failures may stun us with our own inadequacy but they can also, as Teresa of Avila says, knock grace into us.

When there is nothing left in us that can please us or comfort our own minds, when we seem to be useless and worthy of all contempt, when we seem to have failed...it is then that the deep and secret selfishness that is too close for us to identify is stripped away from our souls.

Thomas Merton[88]

Sunshine: Abandonment to God

Lord, I make you a present of myself. I do not know what to do with myself. So let me make this exchange: I will place myself entirely in your hands, if you will cover me.

Lord, I want no special signs from you nor am looking for intense emotions.... Let my love for you be naked, without emotional clothing.

Catherine of Genoa[89]

My second major experience of failure as a mother was even darker than my first. Several years ago I lost a baby when I was fourteen weeks pregnant. This was my fourth miscarriage, but I had three living children who might have comforted me. Yet I was filled with a sense of failure, fear, and despair. A mother's primary duty is to keep her children safe, but I had somehow let my unborn babies die. I became overwhelmed with terror that I would also fail to keep my other children safe. The world's dangers seemed magnified, while my own sense of inadequacy was overpowering.

I'd always depended on my faith in God to help me make sense of the world, and until now my faith had never failed me. I'd been proud of that, as smug and secure in my faith as I had once been in my confidence that I was the perfect mother. But my faith, or at least the thing I had always called faith, was useless to me now. I longed for God, but I could not believe in God's reality. I was in total darkness, and like a child, I was terrified of the dark.

All of us, though, tend to confuse our faith in God with our own self-confidence. When we feel strong and in control, then we can more easily say we trust in God. What we really trust is ourselves. Thomas Merton says,

Self-confidence is a precious natural gift, a sign of health. But it is not the same thing as faith. Faith is much deeper and it must be deep enough to subsist when we are weak,... when our self-confidence is gone, when our self-respect is gone.... True faith must be able to go on even when everything else is taken from us. Only a humble [person] can accept faith on these terms.[90]

Failure forces us to realize our own lack. Without failure our faith would never mature, for we would build even our faith on our own strength rather than on God's. The fourteenth-century anonymous author of *The Cloud of Unknowing* believed that the failure of our human faculties is essential to our spiritual growth. "This cloud and this darkness," the author said, "no matter what you do, is between you and your God. It prevents you from seeing clearly with your mind and from experiencing the sweetness of his love in your heart." What we are left with is only a "naked reaching-out to God."[91]

But we are so impatient, so conditioned to look for immediate results. Blind, surrounded by this cloud, we struggle and thrash, wanting only to get back to the easy, sunlit path we'd been following. But, says the author of *The Cloud of*

Unknowing, "prepare yourself to wait in this darkness as long as you may."[92]

This is the part of our spiritual path that Saint John of the Cross called "the dark night of the soul." It is here, says Saint John, that "God takes you by the hand and guides you in darkness, as though you were blind, along a way and to a place you know not. You would never have succeeded in reaching this place no matter how good your eyes and feet."[93]

Sooner or later, motherhood brings us to this point where we can no longer rely on our own strength and ability. We don't like the dark cloud that surrounds us, for letting go of our self-illusions is painful. Without them, the world is terrifying. We struggle to find some other comfort, some other source of light. When we fail to find anything to restore our sense of security, we sink into depression. But if we wait quietly, "naked," as Catherine of Genoa says, "without any emotional clothing," God finds us even here. Our only hope is to surrender ourselves to Divine love. When we do, the light that bursts upon us is brighter than any we have yet seen.

"These rays," says Catherine, speaking of God's love, "purify and then annihilate. The soul becomes like gold that becomes purer as it is fired, all dross being cast out."[94]

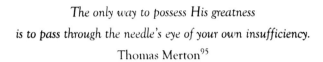

The only way to possess His greatness
is to pass through the needle's eye of your own insufficiency.
Thomas Merton[95]

The Old Testament tells the story of Jacob wrestling in the night with an angel. The angel first wounds him, then both blesses him and gives him a new identity. As mothers, perhaps we can look at our failures as God's angels. In the midst of our darkest nights, God radically touches us, wounding our pride and self-confidence. But God does not leave us there. Instead, when we at last abandon our comforting images, when we allow ourselves to drop naked into the Divine hands, God blesses both us and our children. And then God calls us by our new names, the names that will make us whole, and leads us into the light.

CHAPTER EIGHT

Discipline

"You're acting like you're the center of the world," my husband and I sometimes say to our daughter. As the oldest child, for nearly three years of her life we taught her she *was* the center of our world. Now she has to unlearn that lesson, while we teach her a new outlook. This new point of view is often painful, but sooner or later we all have to learn it. We have to cease to see ourselves as the rulers of our personal kingdoms. Discipline is the thing that shoves us off our thrones.

Like mortification, though, discipline is another word with a bad reputation. We connect it with strict schoolteachers who rapped our knuckles for small offenses; we think of spankings and being sent to bed without supper. In our minds, discipline follows bad behavior. It's the same as punishment.

Actually, though, the word *discipline* comes from the Latin for *teaching* or *learning*. Discipline helps us grow, helps us learn more about ourselves and God. The aspects of motherhood this book discusses are all disciplines. They are patterns of living that instruct our hearts. They teach us that we are not the center of the world.

We submit to motherhood's disciplines, but at the same time we are our children's disciplinarians. No matter how sweet and innocent babies are, they think they are not only the world's center, but the world itself. With our help, their world gets bigger, until at last they find their place in relation to those around them, a place where they are free to both give and take, a place where they can learn their responsibility both to themselves and to others. If this did not happen, if our children kept their infantile outlooks, then they would grow into sociopaths, monsters whose only reality was themselves.

The responsibility we have to teach our children does not mean that we rule them or their behavior. What it does mean is that we help them learn the paths of holiness and health. In the process, we too are being taught.

Being obedient to the disciplines of our lives is not easy, however—not for our children and not for ourselves. At times we are all filled with rebellion. We do not want to submit; we want to control. Discipline puts constraints on our lives when we would rather be free, spontaneous, self-indulgent.

We'd rather grab whatever we want from life. After all, what would be the harm, since God is everywhere and in all things?

As human beings, however, we are limited by our self-centeredness. We need structures that will channel our lives toward God. The alternative only looks like freedom. In reality we are slaves to our egocentric natures. Discipline opens the door to true liberty.

All of us, children and mothers alike, do not pass easily through this door. We all want to be the god of our own lives. We want to be the center of the world.

Shadow: Rebellion

Rules, prudence, subjections...[are] dreadful walls
to a burning soul wild as mine...for me, I am like a fiery horse.
Elizabeth Seton[96]

Even the saints had problems with discipline. We imagine them as bloodless martyrs who possessed no will of their own and delighted in submission, but they were not born holy and selfless any more than we or our children are. Instead, the fiery force of their personalities was channeled by discipline, just as ours must be.

Picture motherly, dedicated Elizabeth Seton as a wild horse bucking and plunging against "rules, prudence, subjugations." Think of Teresa of Avila, an intelligent, competent woman in an age that gave little respect to women. She knew how things should be done, and she probably knew better than the masculine hierarchy. Being a submissive woman irked her so much at times that she wrote, "My Lord, how is it that you command things that seem impossible? As a woman I am constrained on every side in my ambition." She confesses in her autobiography that sometimes she felt so "peevish and ill-tempered" that she wanted to "snap everyone up."[97] And then imagine mild Thérèse of Lisieux all flushed and perspiring as she writes, "I knew it was better to endure patiently" but "sometimes I was soaked with sweat under the strain."[98] The saints understood our rebellion.

This rebellion can be healthy, for rebellion is the thing that says, "It's not fair!" It's what makes us stand up for our rights against forces that would squash us. It's what makes us fight for change.

But much of our rebellion rises from our need to be at the center. When we whine, "It's not fair," a lot of the time we really mean we should have not only our equal share, but the biggest and the best: "I *should* be the center of the world. It's not fair that they won't let me."

When our rebellion clashes with our children's, then as disciplinarians we are no longer successful. Instead we ride a teeter-totter between "They are bad children," and "I am a bad mother." If our children's rebellion makes them "bad," then we are entitled to our anger, our need to control their behavior. But our feelings of aggression against our children make most of us uneasy and then down we go into depression and guilt, as the Good Mother rises up to point her finger at us. Whether we're up or down on this teeter-totter, we are in no position to discipline our children with authority.

Authority is yet another word many of us don't like. Our society is no longer at the far end of the pendulum swing, as it was in the Sixties, when experts recommended absolute permissiveness to parents as they raised children. Still, we've all been influenced by the ideals of freedom and democracy, and we certainly don't want to return to the days when children were to be seen and not heard. Anyway, authority is seldom part of the Good Mother's image.

Christ's perspective on authority was different from ours, though. "Let the person who is the greatest among you become as the youngest," he said, "and the leader as the servant" (Lk 22:26). In other words, authority is not hierarchal and our authority as parents does not come from the fact that we are stronger and our children are weaker. Instead, Jesus put authority in the same realm with service and humility. "Now that I, your Lord and Teacher, washed your feet, you also should wash one another's feet (Jn 13:14). Our authority as mothers comes from our willingness to serve our children in the most ordinary and menial ways.

This concept of authority has less to do with control than it does with love, with teaching a way of life through action. When, as mothers, we follow Christ's example, we are less likely to find our rebellion bumping heads with our children's, for we cannot teach what is not true for ourselves. We can only discipline our children in ways we ourselves experience as real.

As women, though, sometimes we're tired of always being the selfless, giving ones. Sometimes we want to throw a tantrum and be as selfish as our two-year-olds. We have our rights, after all and we're tired of lying on the floor while the entire family wipes their feet on us. We long for freedom. We're sick of being sweet.

John Wesley, the eighteenth-century theologian who founded Methodism, recommended that we allow discipline to build in our natures "humility, meekness, yieldingness, gentleness, sweetness."[99] These sound like feminine qualities, the sort of femininity that nowadays sticks in our throats. But Wesley's system of discipline, his "Methods of Holiness," was not written for women so much as for men. He advocated that all people follow holy lifestyles so that the inner person would be molded into Christ's image. Maybe we women have tended to already demonstrate these qualities because down through the years we have been disciplined by motherhood's methods.

This is a hard attitude to accept, though. The feminist rebellion against women's submissive inferiority was healthy and needed. We don't want to negate it. And besides, many of us are children (or grandchildren) of the Sixties and we like freedom. Like Elizabeth Seton, we feel that rules are "dreadful walls."

Julian of Norwich, the fourteenth-century anchorite, knew all about walls, for she spent her life confined to a tiny cell attached to a church. She was not a prisoner, though. These were walls she selected. With her own free will, she chose to be obedient to restriction.

As mothers, we too have chosen a life of restriction. Our obedience to the limitations of our lives, our love and commitment to our children, is the thing that makes us able not only to discipline ourselves but our children too. If we follow our rebellion, then we will knock down the walls of our own house.

May Sarton says,

...Though we dream of never having a wall against
All that must flow and pass and cannot be caught.
An ever-welcoming self that is not fenced.
Yet we are tethered still to another thought:
The unsheltered cannot shelter, the exposed
Exposes others; the wide-open door
Means nothing if it cannot be closed.

Those who create real havens are not free,
Hold fast, maintain, are rooted, dig deep wells;
Whatever haven human love may be
There is no freedom, without sheltering walls.
And when we imagine wings that come and go
What we see is a house, and a wide open window.[100]

Too often our rebellion makes us pursue an illusion, a make-believe freedom that gets in the way of our real freedom. Our need to be at the center of the world will only enslave us to our own egos. This slavery is sterile and nonproductive. Just as when we follow a recipe, write a poem, do carpentry, or sew a quilt, creativity requires that we work within a framework of rules. Motherhood is like a tree that needs commitment's deep roots—and tethered by those roots we grow. "Obedience," says author Dominic Milroy, "is not an imposed subservience to an external authority but a condition of inward growth."[101]

We are all human; we all rebel. As mothers, though, we cannot afford to spend much time pursuing rebellion's darkness, for we are in the business of sheltering and building homes. Our rebellion would expose our children, put them at risk. Sometimes, though, blinking our eyes against rebellion's black blast, we miss something important: this home of ours has a "wide open window" and we have "wings that come and go." When we choose to turn our backs on rebellion, then we are truly free.

I do not feel the Lord has given me either spirituality or the desire for it.... But, as I know that strength arising from obedience has a way of simplifying things which seem impossible, my will... resolves to attempt this task, although the prospect seems to cause my physical nature great distress.... In His mercy I put my trust.

Teresa of Avila[102]

Sunshine: Obedience to Love

The way of salvation is easy.
It is enough to love.
Margaret of Corona[103]

Margaret of Corona did not say these words glibly. As a single mother during the thirteenth century she faced the world's scorn and condemnation. She had broken the rules, and the price of any worldly redemption was far beyond her means. Her obedience to God's will, however, transformed her life, revealing to her that spirituality comes not from following a specific set of laws but from abandoning ourselves to God's love. "The heaven of heaven is love," wrote John Wesley. "There is nothing higher in religion, there is, in effect, nothing else. If you look for anything but more love, you are looking wide of the mark, you are getting out of the royal way."[104] The way of salvation is easy.

As human beings, though, we like to turn this simple obedience to love into an external legal code. Richard Foster, the author of *Celebration of Discipline*, says that when our discipline deteriorates into law, the result is pride and fear.

Pride takes over because we come to believe that we are the right kind of people. Fear takes over because the power of controlling others carries with it the anxiety of losing control, and the anxiety of being controlled by others.

If we are to progress in the spiritual walk so that the Disciplines are a blessing and not a curse, we must come to the place in our lives where we lay down the everlasting burden of needing to manage others.[105]

This is the load that Demeter could not lay down when it came to letting go of Persephone. As mothers, all of us cling to the same burden. We feel we ought to manage our children's lives, and both our interior discipline of our own hearts and our exterior discipline of our children become a source of pride and fear.

The only solution is to let go of our children, to let go of our own need to be in control. As a result, Margaret of Corona's easy way will also cost us everything. "One cannot love God," Mother Teresa says, "except at the cost of oneself."[106] In fact, we can't love anyone without this same cost. Loving means you give yourself away. This self-giving love disciplines our own hearts, and it's also necessary for our children's discipline. The best discipline is built not on anger, but on loving affirmation.

This will not weaken our discipline. It will not turn us into wishy-washy mothers who allow our children to trample us. The word *affirmation* comes from the Latin *to make firm*. It's not a namby-pamby sort of word. Instead, its demands are rigorous and stringent. When we affirm our children we give them strong, definite outlines. We impose boundaries on their worlds. We allow them to separate from us. We show them who they are in God's eyes.

In the process, we as mothers are also both disciplined and affirmed. We become more whole even as we let go. Just as in pregnancy and birth, we open ourselves to our children, despite the pain. In *If Only I Were a Better Mother*, Melissa Gayle West writes,

> Opening our hearts can mean letting our children make their own mistakes and learn from them. Opening our hearts to our children can mean loving them and ourselves enough to set boundaries that as adults we know they are unprepared to set.... Opening our hearts to our children, with no conditions, does not mean we will always say "Yes" to what they do. It does mean that we will, to the best of our abilities, say "Yes" to who they are.[107]

Motherhood's discipline requires that we say yes not only to our children's identities, but also to God's will as it is expressed in the present moment. Whether communion or exhaustion, holy play or monotony, mortification or revelation, we affirm whatever is. Rebellion turns away from the present's reality, obedience says, "Yes." "These things," says John Wesley, "far from being hindrances to your soul are profitable, yea, necessary for you. Therefore receive them from God (not from chance) with willingness, with thankfulness."[108]

This thankful "yes" comes easier some times than others. Sometimes it takes all our strength not to say "no." Our obedience is not passive but active, and motherhood's path to holiness is not one of weakness. It asks that we pour all the force of our personality into our obedience. As Mother Teresa says,

> Often, under the pretext of humility, of trust, of abandonment, we can forget to use the strength of our will. Everything depends on these words: "I will" or "I will not." And into the expression "I will" I must put all my energy."[109]

When we say "Yes" to love, then motherhood's light and shadow unites our hearts with God. The process is no magic spell that changes us against our will, nor does it suppress our own initiative. Instead, we exercise both our freedom and our willpower, consenting to love's transformation.

He will continue (as He has begun)
to work in a gentle and almost insensible manner.
Let Him take His own way.
He is wiser than you; He will do all things well.
John Wesley[110]

Like a lens, discipline imposes order on our lives, focusing them so we see God's light. Discipline is not an end in itself. In other words, it is not a set of bleak external laws that restricts our lives. Instead, it is a method for achieving our goal: wholeness, holiness, the Presence of God.

CONCLUSION

Journey's End

What we call the beginning is often the end.
And to make an end is to make a beginning.
The end is where we start from.
T.S. Eliot[111]

When we were children, motherhood may have looked like a safe sanctuary at the end of youth's road, the happily-ever-after where we would live the rest of our lives. Some day, all good little girls knew, we would find in motherhood's sunshine an identity that would be always loving, nurturing, and good, and we would hug tight our joy in our children and whisper, "Mine."

We were wrong. From the moment we become pregnant, we plunge in and out of cycles of light and dark, birth and death, beginnings and endings. Motherhood turns out to be not the warm haven at the end of our path, but only a way of journeying along that path, a way that leads through stretches of both sunshine and shadows. It is a way that will ultimately grow fainter and fainter, forcing us to find new paths. As T. S. Eliot says, "The end is where we start from."

As human beings, though, we like to cling and clutch. After all, we have found God in this path called motherhood. How can God ask us to leave behind the place where we have seen the Divine face? Like Peter at the Transfiguration, we'd like to build a permanent construction around this revelation. We'd like to dwell here permanently. And just as Christ told Peter, we can't. Life won't let us. Our children won't let us. Once again we have to let go.

Charles Williams, one of the other authors in C. S. Lewis's group the Inklings, said our prayer should always be, "This too is Thou. Neither is this Thou."[112] In other words, we can find God in all things—and yet the Divine is too big to be contained. When we try to pin God down, when we try to make rules and assumptions about the Divine presence, then we are left with a small, safe god of our own making. God transcends our boxes.

Motherhood requires that we become flexible, that we learn to perfect one pattern of life—and then to relinquish that pattern to make room for another. It asks that we learn to inhabit the present moment, rather than either the past or the present. William Blake said,

> He who binds to himself a joy
> Does the winged life destroy;
> But he who kisses the joy as it flies
> Lives in eternity's sunrise.[113]

As mothers, we cherish each bright moment and then we have to let it go.

We have to let the dark moments go too, for we cannot touch the Divine in our guilt about the past any more than we can find God in nostalgia for yesterday's sunshine. By the same token, we can't hope to find the Divine Presence in our anxiety about what lies ahead. "I AM"—being, first person, present tense—is the Divine name, and God touches us now, in the present moment, whatever it holds: blazing triumph or somber failure, glowing contentment or murky frustration, dazzling joy or pitch-black grief. "Be like the lilies of the field," Christ said (Lk 12:27), and instead of lilies, I think of dandelions, those cheery little flowers that fill our fields. No matter how many times we mow off their yellow heads, they grow back again, their tough little roots dug deep in the here and now, their petals wide to catch the sun. As mothers, we often try to hug that ray of sunlight, instead of simply opening ourselves to it. We can't hold it, though, any more than we can capture a shadow. Almost automatically, however, we try to build permanent homes from our lives' fleeting light and shade, and even when the house is empty, we'd like to keep the walls intact.

God asks us to be pilgrims, though, spiritual vagabonds rather than homebodies. The Divine One asks us to keep walking (Mi 6:8). The metaphor of walking seems safe enough, but we have forgotten what all toddlers know and what we may realize again as older women: walking is risky. David Steindl-Rast notes that walking requires, "a constant losing and finding of our balance."[114]

We don't like to be always in the process of losing and finding anything; we'd much rather just find something and hold on to it. Even when motherhood's dramas are far from pleasant, we'd still rather inhabit them fully, dwelling on them, fretting and worrying, making them *ours*. Anything rather than let go.

When we finally do let go, though, God's gift to us is "the peace that passes all understanding" (Phil 4:7). "I have calmed and quieted my soul," says Psalm 131:2, "like a child quieted at its mother's breast." God, like any good-enough mother, picks us up when we fail, steadies us when we falter, and keeps on loving us no matter how many times we stumble. God understands that learning to walk is hard and scary work.

And sometimes this work hurts. Ultimately, letting go means that we must also let go of our demands that our lives be pain-free. During labor, we learned to be obedient to pain's rhythm, to work with it, and as we walk through motherhood's dark-and-light patterns, we are reminded of that lesson. It's a bleak lesson, a night-black one, but as mothers, most of us are forced to realize something else as well: the time comes to grow up.

No matter how old we are when we enter motherhood (and more and more of us are in our thirties or even forties when we have our first child), we still think like children, seeing ourselves as the center of the world, believing we somehow *deserve* only sunshine in our lives. Motherhood is a rite of passage, though. It thrusts us out of our own childhood and rearranges forever our position in the world.

That world holds pain and darkness. We can't deny it anymore, can't run away and play so we won't have to think about it. Even our brightest joys are shadowed by sorrow. We don't like pain and we're not asked to like it. But somehow during those black times, pain washes away the ordinary, selfish dirt that keeps us from seeing eternity's light. What's more, pain unites us with Christ's suffering, makes us one with his ongoing life. "Unless a kernel of wheat falls to the ground and dies, it remains only a single seed. But if it dies it produces many seeds" (Jn 12:24). Brokenness and fruitfulness, pain and growth, death and birth dance together hand in hand, dependent on each other.

Motherhood's everyday cycles of dying and birth mean that as mothers we are always in the process of being transformed, even while we are always dying to our old selfish selves. It's not easy—but the saints all knew that only *asceticism* leads to holiness and wholeness (the word asceticism means hard work, discipline, and self-denial, all aspects of motherhood's path). No one ever said it would be easy, not even Christ. Yet Christ, the one who gave himself most completely, is also the one who said his own joy would be ours, permanently (Jn 16:22).

Mary, a mother like the rest of us, must have understood this checkered pattern of light and dark we all experience. Her understanding of the Incarnation would have been real and intimate, for like all mothers she had written in her heart the days when she cared constantly for her child's needs, those days when each hour was filled with a hundred tangible acts of love: wiping a food-streaked face, stuffing small arms through sleeves, drying a little body fresh from the bath. Unfortunately, in our world of injustice, disease, and catastrophe, the cost of incarnation—the shadow cast by having a body—is immense and dark. Mary watched her child pay that cost, and one way or another, so do the rest of us mothers.

When we do, the dark seems unbearable, but Jesus said that we live on "every word that proceeds from the mouth of God" (Mt 4:4). David Steindl-Rast reminds us that Christ said every word, not just the pleasant ones like "communion," "rest," and "play," but the dark words such as "exhaustion," "loss," and even "death." Even these words feed us. As mothers, the thought of death is terrifying: our own because our children need us, and theirs because we cannot imagine life without them. But Steindl-Rast goes on to say,

> From our partial experiences of dying...we learn that faith is the power to die into greater aliveness every time we get killed. And so we have reason to expect that being fully killed will mean coming fully alive.[115]

Like all the other cycles of our path, the ease with which we grasp this, the confidence with which we walk, and our sense of our own faith come and go. Sometimes a lesson we thought we'd never forget must be learned all over again farther down the road, and each time around we break a little more, just like the husk of that seed Jesus talked about.

No matter how bright our sunlit moments, we can't escape the pain and breaking, the darkness and shadows. The only way we can bear them is by keeping our eyes fixed on eternity. Our belief in a light that's everlasting makes even our shadows flicker with new meaning. All that we experience as mothers is somehow part of a greater, fuller reality of which we can only catch glimpses now. In that eternal reality, in *kairos*, God somehow keeps safe the things we love. "I...am convinced that he is able to guard what I have entrusted to him," says 2 Timothy 1:12. Nothing we give to God is permanently lost, only transformed.

Julian of Norwich, in one of her visions, realized the safety and permanence of God's love:

It seemed to me that it might fall into nothingness, it was so small. An answer was given to my understanding. "It lasts and ever shall last, because God loves it."[116]

Like our children, we long for security, but motherhood, with all its aspects and stages, makes us realize that God is the only answer to that longing. God is the only true safety—the one still point in the turning world, as T. S. Eliot put it in his poem *Burnt Norton*.[117] In God alone there is no shadow of turning (Jas 1:17).

Our day-to-day dependence on God's eternal love is the same as the saints experienced. Like them, we have committed ourselves to a way of life that disciplines our deep-rooted egotism. We have laid down our own lives and consecrated ourselves to love's demands.

The word *consecrate* has the same Latin root as the word *sacrifice*. They both mean *to make sacred*. As mothers, our lives are sewn together with sacred moments, moments that call us out from ourselves into God's presence. We cannot do this alone. We need the context of our families to create the altar for our sacrifice, the community of our consecration.

Says Evelyn Underhill:

What is being offered you is...a larger and intenser life, a career, a total consecration.... This life shall not be abstract and dreamy, made up, as some imagine of negations. It shall be violently practical and affirmative.... It shall cost much, making perpetual demands on your loyalty, trust, and self-sacrifice.... But you will find in all that happens to you, all that opposes and grieves you—even in those inevitable hours when...the cruel tangles of the world are all that you can discern—an inward sense of security.[118]

This sense of security is the glowing heart of our patchwork lives. It is what enables us to say, as Mary did when she became pregnant with Jesus, "Let it happen to me according to Your will" (Lk 1:38).

We too are pregnant with new creation, the ongoing creation of the selves God has called us to be. In *Green Dolphin Street*, one of Elizabeth Goudge's characters says, "You were born again, my daughter, you escaped from the weight of the old self.... Though you did not realise it the new self was growing as a child in the womb during the time of chaos; destruction and construction always go hand in hand...they will go on through your whole life."[119] This lifelong journey of ours seems sometimes to lead us in circles, in and out of sun and dark, destruction and construction, but like Mary we say "yes" in obedience and trust, "yes" to both the light and darkness in our lives, knowing that both we and our children are growing, held safe in God's hands.

One day, we'll be born out of this world's darkness into light eternal. But in the meantime, motherhood's disciplines teach us the hard paradox of Christ's promise: "Whoever finds his life will lose it, and whoever loses his life for my sake will find it" (Mt 10:39).

The demand of this paradox is sharp and unrelenting, for this is no soft, easy path we've chosen. As on those Amish quilts, the light is brilliant and intense, the shadows dark and jagged. And yet God has also promised to "gently lead those that have young" (Is 40:11); God is with us, the Divine face revealed in each of motherhood's stages. God loves us unconditionally, just as our young children love us.

And as we piece together motherhood's contrasting fabrics, we too give God our love. Elizabeth Seton refers to getting up in the night with her children as "midnight Te Deums." The "Te Deum" is a Latin song of praise that means, "To You, God," and our lives as mothers are filled with this song. Each small selfless act, each acceptance of restriction, God receives with love.

I have a vision of all the [mothers] gathered before God on judgement day. The Lord will say to us: "I was hungry and you fed me, thirsty and you gave me a drink, naked and you clothed me, homeless and you sheltered me, imprisoned and you visited me...."

And we will interrupt, protesting. "Not I, Lord. When did I see you hungry and feed you?"

And the Lord will say: "How could you ask, you of the three-and-a-half-million peanut butter and jelly sandwiches!"

"But thirsty, Lord?"

"I was in the Kool-ade line that came in with the summer heat and the flies, and left fingerprints on your walls and mud on your floors, and you gave me a drink."

"But naked, Lord, homeless?"

"I was born to you naked and homeless, and you sheltered me, first in wombs and then in arms. You clothed me with your love, and spent the next twenty years keeping me in jeans."

"But imprisoned, Lord?"

"Oh, yes. For I was imprisoned in my littleness behind the bars of a crib and cried out in the night, and you came. I was

imprisoned inside a twelve-year-old body that was exploding with so many new emotions, I didn't know who I was anymore, and you loved me into being myself. And I was imprisoned behind my teenage anger, my rebellion, and my stereo set, and you waited outside my locked door for me to let you in.

"Now, Beloved, enter into the joy which has been prepared for you for all eternity."

Kathleen O'Connell Chesto[120]

Saint John the Divine said that Christ is the light that has shone in the darkness from the beginning of time (Jn 1:5). This same light illumines our motherhood. It is the beginning of our spiritual journey—and it waits with love and welcome at our journey's end.

Notes

1. Marge Piercy, "Looking at Quilts," *Circles on Water* (New York: Alfred A. Knopf, 1982).

2. This is a term basic to Winnicott's writings; see D. W. Winnicott, *The Maturational Process and the Facilitating Environment* (Madison, Conn.: Universities Press, 1965) and *Playing and Reality* (New York: Basic Books, 1971).

3. Teresa of Avila, quoted in *The Wisdom of the Saints*, ed. Jill Haak Adels (New York: Oxford University Press, 1987), 205.

4. William Law, *The Joy of the Saints*, ed. Robert Llewelyn (Springfield, Ill.: Templegate Publishers, 1988), 7.

5. Teresa of Avila, quoted in *The Wisdom of the Saints*, ed. Adels, 205.

6. Mecthild of Magdeburg, *The Flowing Light of the Godhead*, trans. Lucie Menzies (London: Longmans, Green, 1953), 3-5.

7. Catherine of Siena, quoted in *The Wisdom of the Saints*, ed. Adels, 204.

8. Marie of the Incarnation, *Selected Writings*, ed. Irene Mahoney (New York: Paulist Press, 1984), 200-212.

9. Margaret Hebblethwaite, *Motherhood and God* (London:

Geoffrey Chapman, 1984), 19–20.

10. Martin Luther, *The Darkness of Faith*, ed. James Atkinson (London: Darton, Longman and Todd, 1987), 82.

11. Julian of Norwich, *Showings*, trans. Edmund Colledge and James Walsh (New York: Paulist Press, 1978), 298.

12. Augustine of Hippo, *The Heart at Rest*, ed. Dame Maura See (Springfield, Ill.: Templegate, 1986), 56.

13. Quoted in Leonard Foley, *Believing in Jesus: A Popular Overview of the Catholic Faith* (Cincinnati, Ohio: St. Anthony Messenger Press, 1980), 99.

14. Julian of Norwich, *Enfolded in Love*, ed. Robert Llewelyn, trans. Sheila Upjohn (London: Darton, Longman, and Todd, 1980), 36.

15. Julian of Norwich, *Showings*, 298.

16. Amedee Brunot, *Mariam: The Little Arab*, trans. Jeanne Dumais and Sister Miriam of Jesus (Eugene, Ore.: The Carmel of Maria Regina, 1990), 48.

17. Katherine Gieve, *Balancing Acts: On Being a Mother* (London: Virago, 1989), ix.

18. Catherine of Genoa, *Purgation and Purgatory, The Spiritual Dialogue*, trans. Serge Hughes (New York: Paulist Press, 1979), 129.

19. Carol Lee Flinders, *Enduring Grace: Living Portraits of*

Seven Women Mystics (New York: HarperCollins, 1993), 149.

20. Elizabeth Seton, *Elizabeth Seton, Selected Writings*, ed. Erin Kelly and Annabelle Mellville (Mahwah, N.J.: Paulist Press, 1987), 222.

21. Therese of Lisieux, *The Story of a Soul: The Autobiography of St. Therese of Lisieux.*, trans. John Beevers (New York: Doubleday, 1989), 99–100.

22. Julian of Norwich, *Showings*, 301.

23. William Blake, *The Poems of William Blake*, ed. William Butler Yeats (New York: Book League of America, 1938), 90.

24. Seton, 347.

25. Mother Teresa of Calcutta, *The Love of Christ: Spiritual Counsels*, ed. Georges Gorree and Jean Barbier (San Francisco: Harper & Row, 1982), 111.

26. Evelyn Underhill, *The Spiritual Life* (New York: Harper & Row, n.d.), 60.

27. Elizabeth of the Trinity, *The Complete Works of Elizabeth of the Trinity, vol. 2*, trans. Anne Englund Nash (Mt. Carmel, Wash.: ICS Publications, 1996), letter 298.

28. Teresa of Avila, *Living Water*, ed. Sister Mary Eland (Springfield, Ill.: Templegate, 1985), 60.

29. Thomas Merton, *The Sign of Jonas* (New York: Harcourt, Brace, 1953), 249.

30. Mother Teresa of Calcutta, 38.

31. Merton, *The Sign of Jonas*, 262.

32. Raymond of Capua, *The Life of Saint Catherine of Siena*, trans. George Lamb (Chicago: P.J. Kenedy & Sons, 1960), 43.

33. Teresa of Avila, as quoted in *Making Prayer Real* by Lynn J. Radcliffe (New York: Abingdon-Cokesbury, 1952), 214.

34. Catherine De Hueck Doherty, *Poustinia: Christian Spirituality if the East for Western Man* (Notre Dame: Ave Maria Press, 1974), 23.

35. Elizabeth of the Trinity, letter 273.

36. Underhill, *The Spiritual Life*, 131.

37. Teresa of Avila, *The Letters of Saint Teresa of Jesus*, trans., ed. E. Allison Peers (New York: Burns & Oates, 1951), Letters 168, 203.

38. Richard J. Foster, *Celebration of Discipline* (New York: Harper & Row, 1978), 138.

39. Margery Kempe, *The Book of Margery Kempe*, trans. B. A. Windeatt (London: Penguin Books, 1985), 252.

40. John Wesley, *The Gift of Love*, ed. Arthur Skevington

Wood (Springfield, Ill.: Templegate, 1987), 75.

41. Anna Maria Taigi, quoted in *The Wisdom of the Saints*, ed. Adels, 173.

42. Jessica Benjamin, *The Bonds of Love* (London: Virago, 1990), 21.

43. Dolores Leckey quotes this unpublished poem by Nancy Joyce in *The Ordinary Way: A Family Spirituality* (New York: Crossroad, 1982), 24.

44. Julian of Norwich, *Enfolded in Love*, 46.

45. Augustine of Hippo, 67.

46. Referred to at length in: Betty Friedan, *The Second Stage* (New York: Dell, 1991).

47. Anne Morrow Lindbergh, *War Within and Without* (New York: Harcourt Brace Jovanovich, 1973), 130.

48. Teresa of Avila, *The Life of Saint Teresa of Jesus*, trans. and ed. E. Allison Peers (New York: Image Books, 1991), 123.

49. Underhill, *The Spiritual Life*, 131–132.

50. Susanna Wesley, *The Prayers of Susanna Wesley*, ed. W. L. Doughty (Grand Rapids, Mich.: Zondervan. 1984), 17.

51. Julian of Norwich, *Enfolded in Love*, 39.

52. Brother Lawrence of the Resurrection, *The Practice of the Presence of God* (Old Tappan, N.J.: Revell, 1958), 9.

53. Cohen, Steve, *Just Juggle* (New York: McGraw-Hill, 1982), 12.

54. Thérèse of Lisieux, 109.

55. Brother Lawrence of the Resurrection, 9.

56. Underhill, *The Spiritual Life*, 132.

57. Cohen, 12.

58. Ibid., 33.

59. Underhill, *The Spiritual Life*, 108.

60. David Steindl-Rast, *Gratefulness, the Heart of Prayer* (Ramsey, N.J.: Paulist Press, 1984), 68.

61. Ibid., 180.

62. John Wesley, 76.

63. Teresa of Avila, *Living Water*, 64.

64. Underhill, *The Spiritual Life*, 134–135.

65. Cohen, 9.

66. Dorothy Day, *Thérèse* (Springfield, Ill.: Templegate, 1979), 3.

67. Cohen, 54.

68. Eugene Warren, from: *Christographia* (St. Louis, Mo.: The Cauldron Press, 1977), 31.

69. See Friedan, 1991.

70. Teresa of Avila, *Living Water*, 64.

71. Taylor, Brian C., *Spirituality for Everyday Living*

(Collegeville, Minn.: Liturgical Press. 1989), 13–14.

72. Merton, *The Sign of Jonas*, 238.

73. Casey, Michael, "St. Benedict's Approach to Prayer," *Cistercian Studies* (1980), 339.

74. Goudge, Elizabeth, *Green Dolphin Street* (London: Hodder and Stoughton, 1956), 92.

75. Brother Lawrence of the Ressurrection, *An Oratory of the Heart* (London: Darton, Longman and Todd, 1984), 163.

76. Bonhoeffer, Dietrich, *Life Together* (New York: Harper & Row, 1952), 77–78.

77. Mother Teresa of Calcutta, 70.

78. Taylor, Jeremy, "The Rule and Exercises of Holy Living," in *Fellowship of the Saints: An Anthology of Christian Devotional Literature* (New York: Abingdon-Cokesbury Press, 1957), 353.

79. Mother Teresa of Calcutta, 112.

80. Thérèse of Lisieux, 89.

81. Wendell Berry, *Collected Poems*, 1957–1982 (San Francisco: North Point Press, 1985), 107.

82. Teresa of Avila, source unknown.

83. Concepción Cabrera de Armida, *Conchita: A Mother's Spritual Diary*, ed. M. M. Philipon, trans. Aloysius J.

Owens (Staten Island, N.Y.: Alba House, 1978), 8.

84. Ibid., 7.

85. Seton, 223-224.

86. George MacDonald, *George MacDonald, An Anthology,* ed. C. S. Lewis (New York: Macmillan, 1978), 8, 10.

87. Robert Farrar Capon, *The Mystery of Christ...& Why We Don't Get It* (Grand Rapids, Mich.: Eerdmans, 1993), 128.

88. Thomas Merton, *New Seeds of Contemplation* (New York: New Directions, 1972), 288.

89. Catherine of Genoa, *The Life and Sayings of Catherine of Genoa,* trans., ed. Paul Garvin (Staten Island, N.Y.: Alba House, 1964), 116.

90. Merton, *New Seeds of Contemplation,* 187.

91. From *The Cloud of Unknowing* as quoted in *All Shall Be Well,* Robert Llewelyn (New York: Paulist Press, 1982), 94-96.

92. Ibid., 95.

93. St. John of the Cross, *The Collected Works of St. John of the Cross,* trans. Kieran Kavanaugh and Otilio Rodriguez (Garden City, N.Y.: Doubleday, 1964), 365.

94. Catherine of Genoa, *Purgation and Purgatory, The Spiritual Dialogue,* 79.

95. Merton, *New Seeds of Contemplation*, 209.

96. Seton, 30.

97. Teresa of Avila, *The Life of Teresa of Jesus*, trans., ed. E. Allison Peers (New York: Doubleday, 1991), 316, 322.

98. Thérèse of Lisieux, 142.

99. John Wesley, 89.

100. May Sarton, "Of Havens," *Recovering: A Journal* (New York: Norton, 1980), 165.

101. Dominic Milroy, "Education According to the Rule of St. Benedict," *Ampleforth Journal*, 89: August 1979), 4.

102. Teresa of Avila, from *The Interior Castle*, Preface, in *The Complete Works of St. Teresa*, trans. E. Allison Peers (London: Sheed & Ward, 1946), 199.

103. Margaret of Corona, *Adels, The Wisdom of the Saints*, 137.

104. Wesley, 54.

105. Foster, 8.

106. Mother Teresa of Calcutta, 21.

107. Melissa Gayle West, *If Only I Were a Better Mother* (Walpole, N.H.: Stillpoint, 1992), 109.

108. John Wesley, 89.

109. Mother Teresa of Calcutta, 20.

110. John Wesley, 42.

111. T. S. Eliot from "Little Gidding" in "Four Quartets,"

The Complete Poems and Plays, 1909–1950 (New York: Harcourt, Brace, World, 1971), 144.

112. Charles Williams. This phrase is used in many of his books, e.g., *War in Heaven, Descent into Hell, The Place of the Lion* (Grand Rapids, Mich.: Eerdmans).

113. Blake, 119.

114. Steindl-Rast, 148.

115. Ibid.

116. Julian of Norwich, *Showings,* 183.

117. Eliot, 119.

118. Evelyn Underhill, *Practical Mysticism* (New York: E. P. Dutton, 1915), 168–169.

119. Goudge, 281.

120. Kathleen O'Connell Chesto, *Why Are the Dandelions Weeds?* (Kansas City, Mo.: Sheed & Ward, 1993), 146–147.

Select Bibliography

Adels, Jill Haak, ed. *The Wisdom of the Saints*. New York: Oxford University Press, 1987.

Augustine of Hippo. *The Heart at Rest*. Ed. Dame Maura See. Springfield, Ill.: Templegate, 1986.

Benjamin, Jessica. *The Bonds of Love*. London: Virago, 1990.

Berry, Wendell. *Collected Poems, 1957–1982*. San Francisco: North Point Press, 1985.

Blake, William. *The Poems of William Blake*. Ed. William Butler Yeats. New York: Book League of America, 1938.

Bonhoeffer, Dietrich. *Life Together*. New York: Harper & Row, 1952.

Brunot, Amadee. *Mariam: The Little Arab*. Trans. Jeanne Dumais and Sister Miriam of Jesus. Eugene, Ore: The Carmel of Maria Regina, 1990.

Capon, Robert Farrar. *The Mystery of Christ...& Why We Don't Get It*. Grand Rapids, Mich.: Eerdmans, 1993.

Catherine of Genoa. *The Life and Sayings of Catherine of Genoa*. Trans., ed. Paul Garvin. Staten Island, N.Y.: Alba House, 1964.

Catherine of Genoa. *Purgation and Purgatory, Spiritual Dialogue*. Trans. Serge Hughes. New York: Paulist Press, 1979.

Catherine of Siena. *The Dialogue.* Trans. Suzanne Noffke. Mahwah, N.J.: Paulist Press, 1980.

The Cloud of Unknowing. Ed. Robert Llewellyn. London: Darton, Longman and Todd, 1983.

Cabrera de Armida, Concepción. *Conchita: A Mother's Spiritual Diary.* Ed. M. M. Philipon, trans. Aloysius J. Owens. Staten Island, N.Y.: Alba, 1978.

Casey, Michael. "St. Benedict's Approach to Prayer." *Cistercian Studies,* 1980, 339.

Chesto, Kathleen O'Connell. *Why Are the Dandelions Weeds?* Kansas City, Mo.: Sheed & Ward, 1993.

Cohen. Steve. *Just Juggle.* New York: McGraw-Hill, 1982.

Day, Dorothy. *Therese.* Springfield, Ill.: Templegate, 1979.

De Hueck Doherty, Catherine. *Poustinia: Christian Spirituality of the East for Western Man.* Notre Dame, Ind.: Ave Maria Press, 1974.

Elizabeth of the Trinity. *Elizabeth of the Trinity: The Complete Works.* Trans. Aletheia Kane. Washington, D.C.: I.C.S. Publications, 1984.

Eliot, T.S. *The Complete Poems and Plays.* 1909–1950. New York: Harcourt, Brace, World, 1971.

Fellowship of the Saints: An Anthology of Christian Devotional Literature. New York: Abingdon-Cokesbury Press, 1957.

Flinders, Carol Lee. *Enduring Grace: Living Portraits of Seven Women Mystics*. New York: HarperCollins, 1993.

Foley. Leonard. *Believing in Jesus: A Popular Overview of the Catholic Faith*. Cincinnati. Ohio: St. Anthony Messenger Press, 1980.

Foster, Richard J. *Celebration of Discipline*. New York: Harper & Row, 1978.

Friedan, Betty. *The Second Stage*. New York: Dell, 1991.

Gieve. Katherine. *Balancing Acts: On Being a Mother*. London: Virago, 1989.

Goudge, Elizabeth. *Green Dolphin Street*. London: Hodder and Stoughton, 1956.

Hebblethwaite, Margaret. *Motherhood and God*. London: Geoffrey Chapman, 1984.

Jewkes, Wilfred T., and Jerome B. Landfield. *Joan of Arc: Fact, Legend, and Literature*. New York: Harcourt, Brace, and World, 1964.

John of the Cross. *The Collected Works of St. John of the Cross*. Trans. Kieran Kavanaugh and Otilio Rodriguez. Garden City, N.Y.: Doubleday, 1964.

Julian of Norwich. *Enfolded in Love*. Ed. Robert Llewellyn. Trans. Sheila Upjohn. London: Darton, Longman, and Todd, 1980.

Julian of Norwich. *Showings.* Trans. Edmund Colledge and James Walsh. New York: Paulist Press, 1978.

Kempe, Margery. *The Book of Margery Kempe.* Trans. B. A. Windeatt. London: Penguin Books, 1985.

Law, William. *A Serious Call to a Devout and Holy Life.* Nashville, Tenn.: Upper Room Press, 1952.

Lawrence of the Resurrection, Brother. *The Practice of the Presence of God.* Old Tappan, N.J.: Revell, 1958.

Lawrence of the Resurrection, Brother. *An Oratory of the Heart.* London: Darton, Longman, and Todd, 1984.

Leckey, Dolores. *The Ordinary Way: A Family Spirituality.* New York: Crossroad, 1987.

Lindbergh, Anne Morrow. *War Within and Without.* New York: Harcourt Brace Jovanovich, 1973.

Llewelyn, Robert. *All Shall Be Well.* New York: Paulist Press, 1982.

———, ed. *The Joy of the Saints.* Springfield, Ill.: Templegate, 1988.

Lord, Bob and Penny. *Saints and Other Powerful Women in the Church.* Westlake Village, Calif.: Journeys of Faith, 1989.

Luther, Martin. *The Darkness of Faith.* Ed. James Atkinson. London: Darton, Longman, and Todd, 1987.

MacDonald, George. *George MacDonald, An Anthology*. Ed. C.S. Lewis. New York: Macmillan, 1978.

Marie of the Incarnation. *Marie of the Incarnation, Selected Writings*. Ed. Irene Mahoney. New York: Paulist, 1989.

Mechthild of Magdeburg. *The Flowing Light of the Godhead*. Trans. Lucie Menzies. London: Longman, Green, 1953.

Milroy, Dominic. "Education According to the Rule of St. Benedict." *Ampleforth Journal*, 89:(August 1979), 4.

Merton, Thomas. *New Seeds of Contemplation*. New York: New Directions, 1972.

Merton, Thomas. *The Sign of Jonas*. New York: Harcourt, Brace and Company, 1953.

Mother Teresa of Calcutta. *The Love of Christ: Spiritual Counsels*. Ed. Georges Gorree and Jean Barbier. San Francisco: Harper & Row, 1982.

Parker, Rozsika. *Mother Love, Mother Hate: The Power of Maternal Ambivalence*. New York: Basic Books, 1995.

Piercy, Marge. *Circles on the Water*. New York: Alfred A. Knopf, 1982.

Radcliffe, Lynn J. *Making Prayer Real*. New York: Abingdon-Cokesbury, 1952.

Raymond of Capua. *The Life of Catherine of Siena*. Ed. George Lamb. Chicago: P.J. Kenedy & Sons, 1960.

Sarton, May. *Recovering: A Journal.* New York: Norton, 1980.

Seton. Elizabeth. *Elizabeth Seton, Selected Writings.* Ed. Erin Kelly and Annabelle Mellville. Mahwah, N.J.: Paulist Press, 1987.

Steindl-Rast, David. *Gratefulness, the Heart of Prayer.* Ramsey, N.J.: Paulist Press, 1984.

Taylor, Brian C. *Spirituality for Everyday Living.* Collegeville, Minn.: Liturgical Press, 1989.

Teresa of Avila. *The Complete Works of St. Teresa.* Trans., E. Allison Peers. London: Sheed & Ward, 1946.

——. *Living Water.* Ed. Sister Mary Eland. Springfield, Ill.: Templegate, 1985.

——. *The Letters of Saint Teresa of Jesus.* Trans., ed. E. Allison Peers. New York: Burns Oates, 1951.

——. *The Life of Saint Teresa of Jesus.* Trans., ed. E. Allison Peers. New York: Doubleday, 1991.

Thérèse of Lisieux. *The Story of a Soul: The Autobiography of St. Thérèse of Lisieux.* Trans. John Beevers. New York: Doubleday, 1989.

Underhill. Evelyn. *The Spiritual Life.* New York: Harper & Row, n.d.

——. *Practical Mysticism.* New York: E.P. Dutton, 1915.

Warren, Eugene. *Christographia*. St. Louis, Mo.: The Cauldron Press, 1977.

Wesley, John. *The Gift of Love*. Ed. Arthur Skevington Wood. London: Darton, Longman and Todd, 1987.

Wesley, Susanna. *The Prayers of Susanna Wesley*. Ed. W. L. Doughty. Grand Rapids, Mich.: Zondervan, 1984.

West, Melissa Gayle. *If Only I Were a Better Mother*. Walpole, N.H.: Stillpoint, 1992.

Winnicott, D. W. *The Maturational Process and the Facilitating Environment*. Madison, Conn.: International Universities Press, 1965.

———. *Playing and Reality*. New York: Basic Books, 1971.

More Books from Ellyn Sanna

All Shall Be Well:
**A Modern-Language Version of
the Revelation of Julian of Norwich**
Julian of Norwich (Ellyn Sanna)
ISBN: 978-1-933630-83-0

The great spiritual classic by Julian of Norwich is now available in modern, easy-to-comprehend language that stays true to Julian's original meanings. Her ancient wisdom is as relevant now as it was in the 14th century's world of plague, prejudice, and war. Discover Julian's joyous affirmation of the certainty of Divine love, a love that overcomes all.

"Julian would be pleased with this rendering of the *Showings* into contemporary English. The even-handed blending here of simple language and the grandeur of Julian's content is flawless; and the happy result is that the *Showings* slip in our minds and hears as effortlessly as if the mystic of Norwich were speaking to us herself, face-to-face and soul-to-soul."
—Phyllis Tickle, founding editor of *Publishers Weekly* Religion Department

"*All Shall Be Well* does for Julian of Norwich what *The Message* did for the Bible....This book is a great introduction to Julian's world for those who are new to her writing, but it's full of insight even for those who know her well.
—Carl McColman, author of *The Big Book of Christian Mysticism*

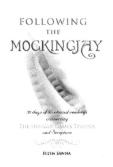

Following the Mockingjay: 30 Days of Devotional Readings Connecting the Hunger Games Trilogy and Scripture
Ellyn Sanna
ISBN: 978-1-937211-64-6

Millions of people are in love with Suzanne Collins' Hunger Games trilogy. Something in these books speaks to both young adults and older people. Despite all the violence and ugliness in the books' post-apocalyptic world, Katniss's mockingjay calls us to justice and compassion. It shows us how to become the people we were created to be. In fact, its message is a lot like the Good News Jesus brings us!

This devotional book allows young adults (and older folks as well) to see the parallels between the Hunger Games trilogy and Scripture. It's ideal for personal devotions, Sunday school classes, and youth groups.

Touching God:
Experiencing Metaphors
for the Divine
Ellyn Sanna
ISBN: 978-1-933630-93-9

This is a gentle invitation to an experience of God that is immediate and intimate. Drawing from both her own life and a range of sources, Ellyn Sanna shows how the lived symbol is often more truly felt than the theology behind it. A profound awareness of this helps us counter a cold, abstract image of God and make all of life sacramental. Beautifully written, *Touching God* uses readily grasped symbols for God found in the natural world, such as wind, water, darkness, light, rock, bread, and more. It includes human roles as metaphor, showing God as gardener, housewife, host, child, friend, lover, spouse, and self. It complements the lovely text with quotes from scripture, as well as classic and contemporary spiritual writers. This book is both very personal yet universally embracing while it helps readers find an image of God that speaks to their own deepest experience.

ANAMCHARA BOOKS
BOOKS TO INSPIRE
YOUR SPIRITUAL JOURNEY

In Celtic Christianity, an *anamchara* is a soul friend, a companion and mentor (often across the miles and the years) on the spiritual journey. Soul friendship entails a commitment to both accept and challenge, to reach across all divisions in a search for the wisdom and truth at the heart of our lives.

At Anamchara Books, we are committed to creating a community of soul friends by publishing books that lead us into deeper relationships with God, the Earth, and each other. These books connect us with the great mystics of the past, as well as with more modern spiritual thinkers. They are designed to build bridges, shaping an inclusive spirituality where we all can grow.

You can order our books at **www.AnamcharaBooks.com**. To find out more about Anamchara Books and connect with others on their own spiritual journeys, visit **www.AnamcharaBooks. com** today.

ANAMCHARA BOOKS
220 Front Street
Vestal, New York 13850
(607) 785-1578
www.AnamcharaBooks.com

CPSIA information can be obtained
at www.ICGtesting.com
Printed in the USA
FFOW02n0118090615
13992FF